CLIFFEDGE
ROAD

CLIFFEDGE ROAD

A Memoir

RANDI FINE

©2019 RaFi Publications, LLC. All rights reserved. Any duplication in whole or in part is prohibited without prior express written permission from the author.

For more information, details about upcoming events, and/or related publications, please visit
www.randifine.com

Contact Randi for information about how this book can be used as a fundraiser or a valuable tool to support your non-profit organization.

ISBN 978-1-7044-5791-8

This book is dedicated with gratitude:

To my guardian angels, who with love and infinite wisdom have allowed me to stumble many times, but have always caught me before I fell.

Contents

Disclaimer ix
Introduction xi
Preface xiii

The Final Curtain 1
Dirty Laundry 3
Broken Doors 11
Winning the Contest 14
The Homework Assignment 20
Never Talk to Strangers 23
Too Hideous to Love 28
Booby-Trapped 35
Off the Wall 39
To Sir with Angst 43
A Living Nightmare 50
The Stormy Aftermath 58
Showing Up to My Party 63
Skeletons in the Closet 71
All the Way 74
The Polaroid Picture 77
Comic Relief 80
First and Foremost an Addict 87
Only Shooting Water 91
Willful Disregard 95

Desperate Measures..99
The Backgammon Game... 106
Keith's Red Shoes... 110
No Turning Back 114
A Woman's Touch 117
Unrelenting Drama... 120
The Double Whammy 124
Baby Fever 142
The Man-Cave Charade 146
At the Eleventh Hour.. 149
The Guidance Whisperer 155
Paper Sunglasses.. 159
Escaping the Danger Zone.. 165
Three Stipulations 173
The Final Rescue 178
Sweet Revenge... 186
The Plastic Fruit Stand 191
Glorious Freedom... 194
Gaining Traction 198
Keith Strikes Again 201
The Tragic Letter...207
Flipping the Switch 211
Getting the Get... 216
A Soft Place to Land 221
Fourth of July..224
Meant to Be 228

Postface..231

Disclaimer

The stories revealed in this book are told from my perspective as I remember personally experiencing them. I present them, from the best of my recollection, as true and honest accounts. Factual information is based on letters, records, and journals I kept over the years.

Some names have been changed to preserve the anonymity of the people involved.

Introduction

I believe that there are divine reasons for the pregnant pauses in our lives; the times when our life seems to come to a screeching halt and we are rendered powerless over it. Those are the times we should pay extra close attention to, for those junctures may be the most profound times in our lives. Though painful, those intervals cause us to sit quietly and come face to face with our true selves. They provide tremendous opportunities for our personal growth.

Despair is a lonely, desolate place we have all visited at some point in our lives. While in its depths, it seems to take an immense amount of courage to reach for rose-colored glasses and put them on.

I spent the first thirty years of my life as a pleaser, yielding to everyone else's expectations of me. Convinced that it was inconsiderate to ever put myself first, I continually dismissed my own needs. Having never developed a healthy self-esteem, I based my identity entirely on the ever-changing opinions of others and my interpretation of their reactions to me. My boundaries were undefined; I wavered between unfiltered vulnerability and impenetrable emotional walls. Those were very tumultuous and depressing years for me.

According to research conducted by professionals in the field of psychology, there are common threads that have been traced back to the childhoods of many adults who suffer from co-dependency.

Many had been "pleaser" children who had been conditioned from a young age to believe that they were only good or valuable when compliant with their parents' wishes. Often, those wishes were illogical and confusing.

As children, they felt unduly responsible for their parents' needs and happiness. Healthy emotional boundaries between their parents and themselves were never properly established. They often suffered from depression and/or anxiety in their adolescences, conditions that continued to trouble them well into adulthood.

The codependent syndrome develops over a long period of time. Those who suffer from codependency in their adulthoods have often had erroneously difficult adolescences. But they are largely unaware of their tendencies until their condition impedes their ability to form healthy, stable adult relationships.

I am grateful to say that although I suffered from that confusion for the first thirty years of my life, today, at sixty-one years of age, my life does not resemble that portrayal in any way. But remembering where I came from keeps me humble.

It is my sincere hope that as you peruse the pages of my book you will find my story touching, inspirational, and most importantly, an impetus for healing.

Preface

I first wrote my memoir in 2009 and titled it Fine…ly.

Many things have changed in the last ten years. For one thing, I have become a much better writer. But the completion of my healing process, the most impactful change, truly sparked the rewrite.

Wanting to protect my family of origin in the first version, I washed over the details of my childhood and tiptoed around the truth. Still, it took a lot of courage to expose what I did at the time. I released that book with great trepidation.

We are taught by our abusers not to air our dirty laundry. That is one of the tactics they employ to keep us as emotional hostages.

I fully appreciate and agree that airing our dirty laundry in situations where amends have been made and the abuse has ended is cruel and vindictive. Those who are truly sorry deserve to be released from the guilt of their transgressions.

However, I do not believe we are obligated to protect through our silence those people with whom we have clearly addressed the problem yet refuse to take responsibility for their actions, and those who wish to continue their abusive behavior.

That does not give us the right to exact punishment on people or smear their names. We all tend to form judgments at times, but we should never impose them on others, especially where someone's reputation or freedom may be concerned.

We should instead find it in our hearts to forgive others for their transgressions, no matter their degree of, or lack of, accountability and redemption. Forgiveness does not absolve anyone from responsibility. It is a gift of peace we give ourselves.

I share my story not to relive the past, not to be cruel or vindictive, not because I lack forgiveness or hold a grudge, but because it is my truth. And truth is freedom. It took many years for me to learn that and claim it.

My aspiration through the sharing of my story is to offer hope, encouragement, and validation to others who have gone through or are going through hard times.

The message of this book is three-fold:

- Miracles happen
- Anything is possible
- Never say never

Be ever grateful for tomorrow. You never know what it may bring.

The Final Curtain

....

*All deaths are sudden, no matter how gradual
the dying may be. ~Michael McDowell*

....

As we lay on our backs looking up at the sky, I glanced over at Cammy expecting to see a spark of childish wonderment in her eyes. She had been a delight, as was typically her nature. Instead, her tiny eyelids looked heavy and kept drifting closed. It had been a long day for her.

Almost an hour had passed since the first launching of the fireworks display. With a sense that the grand finale might begin at any moment, we made a split-second decision to pack up our camp and leave a few minutes early. With any luck, we would avoid the torrent of people all trying to exit the park at the same time, hopefully circumventing the impending traffic jam on the only road out of there.

We quickly grabbed our things and then proceeded to forge a pathway through the vast sea of spectators, trying to be as considerate as possible under the circumstances and not to trample on anyone's blanket. Feeling secure in the safety of her Daddy's arms, Cammy laid her sleepy head on his shoulder as we headed for our car.

As we drove home, I turned my head around and peered into

the back seat of the Maxima. Not surprisingly, Cammy had fallen asleep, her head gently resting on the adult-sized seatbelt strap that miniaturized her petite stature by contrast. A perfectly spiraled golden curl lay softly over one eye. I found myself gazing at her for a moment, marveling at her untainted beauty. Though I dreaded the thought of ever having to disturb her, I knew we would be home in less than fifteen minutes. Surely, she would wake up as we transferred her from the car into the house.

"Daddy will carry you upstairs," I said as he lifted her, languid, dazed, and glassy-eyed, out of the car. He carried her up the front walkway and into the house. "Brush your teeth and get ready for bed, and then I will come up to tuck you in and kiss you goodnight."

I stood in the foyer watching as they ascended the staircase. Then, as I turned and faced the unlit kitchen straight ahead, the blinking red light on the answering machine sitting on the kitchen counter caught my eye. I felt it beckoning me with rapidly pulsating, imposing urgency. Curious, but with a sense of inexplicable foreboding, I approached the machine and played the message.

"Keith's dead. Call me the second you get home." She had not identified herself but she didn't need to. I knew the distinct, raspy sound of my ex-mother-in-law's voice very well.

Though predictable and imminent, the news hit me hard. Keith, my thirty-four-year-old ex-husband had died.

The jolting impact of that day, Wednesday, July 4, 1990, would be indelibly pressed on my memory forever.

Dirty Laundry

....

*Remember, as far as anyone knows we're a
nice normal family. ~Homer Simpson*

....

I took my first breath of life on September 4, 1958.
Karen, age seven, and Linda, age five, anxiously awaited the news of my birth, hoping to get the baby sister they had asked for.

My parents who regarded daughters as more desirable than sons, hit the jackpot a third time.

My father sat in the waiting room listening as the doctors announced the birth of one boy after another. He felt like the luckiest guy in the world when the doctor announced that his wife had given birth to a baby girl.

I grew up in a stereotypical 1960's American family. The five of us lived a comfortable middle-class life in a modern suburb of Baltimore County called Pikesville.

My mother stayed at home attending to the needs of her family as did most married women of that era. She took pride in her job as a full-time housewife and mother.

Mom spent most of her time in her kitchen. She prepared a

delicious three-course meal every night and baked all her own cakes and pastries from scratch.

An attractive lady, she always looked well put-together with her crisply-pressed apron, her just-so hairdo, and her long, manicured nails.

My mother never worked outside the home but did a lot of volunteering. She took an active role in our synagogue's sisterhood, often serving on the board and volunteering her time wherever needed.

As a partner in a family business, my father worked long, grueling hours, six days a week at a job he despised to provide our family with everything we needed. The drudgery made him tired and cranky, though unfortunately never wealthy.

A proud and patriotic World War II veteran, Dad hung an American flag outside our house to honor our country on every national holiday.

Passionate, outgoing, and assertive, he strongly voiced his opinion about everything to everyone; both interested and disinterested. If he had something to say, he did not care who wanted to hear it.

My father, trained as a medic in the army, could manage any crisis in a calm, organized manner. He showed up first, pitched in, and helped anyone who needed it. He had rescued several people and saved many lives as both a soldier and civilian.

My parents, both of the Jewish faith, came from completely different upbringings. My mother grew up in a very observant home; my father did not but celebrated his Jewish heritage with great pride.

Jewish artwork or artifacts of some sort hung on every wall of our house. Our kitchen clock had Hebrew letters instead of numbers.

My mother kept a kosher home. We attended synagogue as a family every Sabbath, and my siblings and I each attended Hebrew school for six years; not in place of regular school but in addition to it.

Mom had built her entire identity around being Jewish. That identity either clouded or influenced every thought she had.

She classified every person she met as Jewish or not Jewish. When she spoke of people I did not know, she always indicated whether or not they were Jewish, as if being Jewish made them more acceptable or put them in an elite category.

I remember her pulling her car over on Reisterstown Road, whenever she saw a Yeshiva boy walking by, to offer him a ride. The boys all looked the same: white shirts with tzitzit hanging out the bottom, yarmulkes on their heads, and black pants. She did not know any of them but felt safe picking them up just because they were "good Jewish boys".

My mother somehow inserted the word Jewish into every conversation I had with her; so much so that just hearing the word made my stomach turn. As a result, instead of being embraced by Judaism as my mother hoped, it turned me completely off to the religion.

I did not judge people by their faith or feel superior to them because of the religion I happened to be born into.

I somehow understood from a very young age that many different perspectives on life existed; perspectives my mother either could not or chose not to expose me to.

One thing I knew for sure—I did not want to spend my life peering through her same narrow lens.

My mother often told me as a child that she hoped I would develop a "thicker skin" than she had so life would not be as painful for me as it had been for her. That always struck me as odd. As far as I knew, she had not had an unusually difficult life or complicated childhood.

Mom grew up poor in the Great Depression, but so did everyone else she knew. As the only girl in a male-dominated home, her mother expected her to help with the household chores. A hard life perhaps, but painful seemed like a stretch.

Starting at around nine or ten years old, I began trying to develop the "thick skin" my mother wanted me to have. I sought out problematic people and pursued difficult, sometimes dangerous, situations to test my resilience; though I did it all behind my mother's back.

I certainly did not want to contend with her over-reactions. Whenever she got upset or overwhelmed, she raged and then the entire family paid dearly. So, I experienced whatever I wanted to experience and then worked the problems out on my own.

Hypersensitive to his wife's mood swings and often the target of them, Dad tiptoed around her. He went to great lengths to shield her from the realities and challenges of life because he knew she could not cope with anything. He made her life very easy, though I don't think she appreciated anything he did for her. She treated him horribly.

My father had lost his mother at the age of five and had no memory of her. He had a cold-hearted, neglectful father who never showed him love. Having longed for a mother's love his entire life, he believed that mothers, especially mine, should be worshiped as queens.

He expected me and my siblings to worship her as well. On more than one occasion, Dad wished me or one of my sisters a happy birthday and then urged, "Thank *Mother* for giving birth to you." I cringed every time I heard him say that.

Dad always referred to Mom as "Mother" or "Your Mother". I don't ever remember him referring to her casually as Mom or Mommy.

Whenever Mom wanted attention, she would refer to herself in the third person saying something like, "Your Mother is not feeling well." I always wanted to reply, "Oh, she isn't?" But she forbid us to ever refer to her as "She". That made her furious. She would say, "I am not a *SHE,* I am your *MOTHER!*"

Everything my siblings and I did, good or bad, somehow reflected upon her. She allowed no room for error. If she even thought someone outside our immediate family might get an inkling of our "less than perfect" behavior, she would lament, "What will people think?" or "How can I show my face in public?"

Cliffedge Road

No matter what we did with our lives outside the home and whatever decisions we made, Mom expected to remain front and center in our world, though she never admitted it. Since Dad worshiped the ground she walked on, he saw things no other way.

We found it very difficult to separate from her at the appropriate stages of our development without feeling terribly guilty for hurting her. We had no healthy way to disentangle from the stifling enmeshment of our family and blossom into the individuals we had every right to be.

My mother had an entirely different persona in public than she did in private. To elicit the reaction she desired, she could seamlessly switch from one to the other. I think she may have been the greatest actress that ever lived.

Unaware of her phony facade, everyone adored her. People often sent her letters of appreciation for favors she did for them telling her what a kind, beautiful lady she was. She thrived on that adoration and knew exactly how to obtain it.

As a child, I did not see anything unusual or dysfunctional about my family. I believed every family operated the way mine did. It took over forty years for me to recognize the degree of madness I had grown up with and before I understood the extreme emotional abuse my siblings and I had endured. Looking back, everything about our family life seemed chaotic and confusing.

To add to the insanity, my parents often told me and my siblings that they loved us and would do anything for us. While we desperately wanted to believe what they said, we could not deny that we came second to their relationship. Their enmeshment in each other's drama left no room for anyone else.

My parents also claimed, albeit falsely, that we could tell them anything. They assured us that no matter the situation, they would understand and support us.

But every time we needed support or advice, we wrestled with whether or not to involve them because they often made us feel worse. Mom would fly off the handle and blame someone for what happened, or act sympathetic and understanding to our faces while stockpiling the information to use as ammunition later—sometimes years later. Dad had patience, compassion, and empathy but he told Mom everything we said. We had no one to advocate for us, no one we could trust.

My parents argued more often than not, neither of them bothering to filter their words. They did not seem to care where they argued, what they said, or how they said it.

As a young child, I found their fighting terribly frightening. Time stood still as I watched in silence, waiting for it to end. Never knowing when the outbursts or melodramatics would break out, I lived stressed out and on high alert at all times.

My parents' behavior was nothing short of disgraceful. My mother frequently and shamelessly belittled my father in our presence. It sickened me to watch her deprecate, humiliate and emasculate him while he obediently acquiesced.

When Dad came home from work each evening, she would goad him into fighting the battles she instigated with us that day by calling him a weak, lousy father. Then jumping to her defense, he would yell at us for hurting our mother, never caring to hear our side of the story. Just like a puppet master, she pulled all his strings.

During "peaceful" times, they acted like teenagers in love— holding hands, kissing, and hugging. They often told my siblings and me that no one had a spouse as wonderful as they each had. I grew up with a seriously distorted understanding of romantic love.

From birth, my mother assigned the role of "Golden Child" to me. She never tried to hide her favoritism from the rest of the family. A huge contrast existed between how she treated me and how she treated my sisters. That upset me. I did not want preferential treatment over them. I adored my sisters and could not bear to see them hurt.

The humiliation, criticism and name-calling my sisters constantly endured frequently caused them to run out of the room crying. Several hours of mournful wailing often followed the verbal abuse.

Those sorrowful sounds resonated throughout the entire house, yet neither of my parents ever tried to console them.

Forced to live in constant chaos and drama, desperate for a harmonious home life, I assumed the role of family mediator. No one else in my family seemed rational enough to do it.

My parents never considered the huge burden they allowed their youngest child to shoulder or the traumatic effect it might have on me.

By the time I reached adolescence, I had become proficient at absorbing other people's pain and protecting their feelings while ignoring my own. That pattern endured well into my adulthood, negatively impacting every relationship I had.

As the youngest child, I had the benefit of watching my sisters interact with my mother and learning from their mistakes. I knew exactly what it took to remain in her good graces.

In my mother's eyes, I could do no wrong. She gazed at me all the time as if she had cultivated a perfect specimen. If I got caught doing something wrong, she never allowed me to own the responsibility; she always blamed someone else. My mother refused to see my imperfections. To admit I had imperfections meant she did too.

I never thought of myself as perfect, but I believed others would only accept and love me if I was. Forever striving for that unattainable quest, I remained depressed and disappointed for many years.

My mother told me that my outer beauty would always open doors for me. She never encouraged me to work at anything or develop my inner self in any way because she believed I naturally had what everyone wanted.

She did me a huge disservice. While other kids focused on education, setting goals, and creating the lives they wanted, I sat there waiting for everything to come to me. When things did not go my way, I could not understand why.

The doors that beauty did open for me made my life anything but easy. They caused me heartache and a great deal of trauma.

It is said that "Mother knows best", and many mothers do. But I learned the hard way that every bit of advice mine ever gave me turned out false; much of it detrimental to my wellbeing.

It took over forty years just to begin unraveling the confusion. Even then I had an arduous journey; a steep uphill climb with many pitfalls. My life, built on a house of cards, had no foundation. I had to build it from the ground up—brick by brick.

BROKEN DOORS

....

I cannot think of any need in childhood as strong as the need for a father's protection. ~Sigmund Freud

....

I never felt physically safe in our family home. As I reflect back on why, I understand that my unease had to do more with emotional safety than physical safety.

The house never felt physically safe to me. It had too many ground-level windows for my comfort. Even though curtains or blinds covered every window, I always felt vulnerable and exposed.

Our house had four entryways. The door used most frequently by my family led from the carport into the den. The front door, usually reserved for guests, opened to the living room. We used the side door in the dining room to go out back or sit on the patio, and my father used the laundry room door when he did his gardening, but mostly to take out the trash.

Though inattentive to the emotional safety of his children, my father diligently attended to the physical safety of our home. He installed deadbolts, chains, and/or slide bars on every door for extra protection. The supplemental locks did nothing to alleviate my fear of someone breaking into the house through a window.

As a child, I often had nightmares about a dark, shadowy figure chasing me around the backyard and right up to the patio door.

Most of my childhood dreams involved our home's doors and windows.

The longest-running recurring dream I ever had began in my adolescence and continued into my early forties.

In the dream, I am always standing by one of the four doors. My father is leaving the house and I am saying goodbye to him. Since I will be home alone, I ask him to please make sure the door is securely locked.

He assures me that he is dead-bolt locking the door and that I do not have to worry about my safety. Then he leaves the house and I walk away.

I come back later to check the lock and reassure myself that I am safe. But when I gently touch the doorknob, the entire door opens.

I try to relock the door from the inside but no matter what I do I cannot lock it. I am terrified that someone will come in and hurt me.

I remain by that door policing it for hours, hoping my father will come home soon.

When he finally returns, I tell him how fearful I felt because I could not lock the door. He has no idea what I am talking about. He tells me there is nothing wrong with the lock and then shows me. The door locks perfectly for him.

Unable to convince my father that the lock needs to be repaired, I continue to fear for my safety.

In my early forties, struggling to understand why I suffered from acute anxiety and depression and why I felt emotionally tortured around my parents, I sought out therapy. I had a severe guilt complex for feeling the way I did about them.

I could not connect the dots. My feelings made no sense to me. I had a great husband and two wonderful children. I thought I'd had a normal childhood with two loving parents. But something constantly ate me up inside. I could not deny that I needed help.

In the first session with my therapist, she identified my pain as a boundary issue. I did not understand what she meant by that. I found it difficult to make the connection between boundaries and my pain.

As I worked with her, I began to recognize the emotional enmeshment I'd had with my parents my entire life. They had complete access to my emotions whether physically with them or not. In time, I came to see that I had never formed a separate identity.

She also helped me recognize the emotionally unsafe and bizarre childhood I had grown up in and the ways in which it had impaired my adult life. I learned how to establish healthy emotional boundaries with my parents and in every aspect of my life.

In one of our sessions, she remarked that my mother sounded like a narcissist. I did not understand what she meant and she did not elaborate further. As a licensed therapist, she probably could not diagnose anyone she had not evaluated.

My mother never acted the selfish way I imagined a narcissistic person acting. She never boasted or primped, she acted humble and modest, and she seemed to have a very charitable heart. I had yet to learn about narcissistic personality disorder or covert narcissism.

I put my therapist's comment on the back burner and did not explore it further until a year later when I learned how to use the Internet. That's when it became crystal clear to me. My mother fit the profile to a T.

My therapy lasted for over a year. When the therapy ended, so did the recurring dream. I was forty-two.

Winning the Contest

....

*The trust of the innocent is the liar's
most useful tool. ~Stephen King*

....

From birth until around age seven, I had a terrible fear of men. I trusted a few that I knew well, but a look or touch from most men sent me into full-blown hysteria.

My paternal grandfather rarely saw my face because I often covered it with my arm. If he spoke to me, I dashed behind the nearest chair or table leg to hide.

My reaction probably seemed irrational to those witnessing it and I am pretty sure it embarrassed my parents. But it makes sense to me in retrospect. Whether intuition or premonition, I must have sensed the danger lurking ahead.

With only a two-year age difference between my sisters, they had gone through school nearly back to back. As a result, I had heard the names of many teachers at their high school and had a sense of their personalities.

Both my sisters seemed fond of one particular male Science teacher. They mentioned his name often. I felt as if I knew him.

One afternoon when I answered the kitchen telephone and a friendly man on the other end identified himself as my sister's

Biology teacher, I just assumed it was that same teacher. Karen had already graduated high school so I figured he had called for or about Linda.

It surprised me when he said he had called to talk to me. I could not imagine what he wanted to talk to me about but felt honored that he did. Excited to know more, I listened with great anticipation as he explained the reason for his call.

He said he called to tell me about a contest that the students in my sister's Biology class were having, involving their younger siblings.

I found it curious that Linda had not told me about her class contest or that it involved me. She typically shared that kind of information with me.

He continued on to say that the students did not know exactly when he would call their homes, and cautioned that if Linda heard me talking to him, he would have to disqualify her.

I assured him she would not overhear our conversation because she had not come home yet and wouldn't be home for a few more hours.

He asked if I was home alone, sounding genuinely concerned that I might be. I told him I wasn't. My mother was downstairs doing laundry. He said he was happy to hear that.

Then he asked how I felt about participating in the contest and if I wanted to help my sister win.

I told him the contest sounded like fun and I definitely wanted to help Linda win. I adored her and would have done anything to make her happy.

Excited to get started, I asked him what I needed to do. He did not directly say, just offered more details

He explained that the class had recently started a human sexuality unit. The students had come up with the idea of polling their younger siblings to see which one knew the most about sex.

Upon hearing that word, I emotionally recoiled. My enthusiasm turned to dread. A sick feeling overtook me and I wanted to vomit.

I could not make sense of what I had just heard. I trusted Linda with my life. It was not in her nature to participate in that kind of thing. What confused me even more was that she had always protected me. Now it seemed she was throwing me to the wolves.

I went mute.

The man asked why I had suddenly gotten so quiet.

I didn't respond.

He assured me that he completely understood if the sex topic had made me uncomfortable and that I didn't have to participate in the contest if I did not want to. He suggested that before I made my decision, I take into consideration that he had already spoken to the other siblings and they all had participated. If I backed out, Linda would be the only classmate excluded.

I felt terribly torn. While I wanted nothing to do with the disgusting contest, I did not want to hurt Linda in any way. I knew this could not have been easy for her either and wanted to do whatever I could to support her.

I wondered how the other kids were able to talk about sex when the mere thought of doing so sickened me. They could not have been much older than I was. I wondered if they were just more mature. Even so, I knew I was stronger and more resilient than any of them could possibly be. If they could do it, I decided I could suck it up and do it too.

I agreed to participate and asked him to hold on a minute while I went somewhere private.

Restricted by the length of the coiled cord attached to the kitchen wall telephone, I went as far as I could go into the adjacent dining room, sat down behind the table, and told him he could begin.

In the first round, he asked elementary level questions about body parts that any ten or eleven-year-old could easily answer—not nearly as embarrassing as I thought they would be.

When that round concluded, he assured me I had answered all the questions correctly. He told me I had done very well and asked if I wanted to continue.

Feeling relieved and confident, I told him I did.

He cautioned that the second part might be a little harder than the first and asked if I had a problem with that.

I told him I did not.

Once he began the second round, I understood why he had warned me. The contest took a drastically sharp turn from marginally innocent to hardcore.

With a laid back, matter of fact tone, he began directing me to touch my body in sexual ways and asking me questions about the sensations I experienced.

I felt humiliated and dirty doing the things he asked of me, but believing my feelings were irrelevant, complied with all of it. I just emotionally detached from the mortification and focused on the finish line.

After the second round concluded, he praised me for a job well done. He assured me that I had done much better than any of the other kids and guaranteed that Linda had won the contest.

He thanked me for my participation, told me to have a great rest of the day, and hung up the phone.

I sat there for a few minutes reorienting myself. All things considered, I felt proud to have gotten through the contest and done as well as I had. I knew how happy it would make Linda to know she had won.

Linda had not planned to come home until dinner time, so that's when I decided to share the great news with her.

I did not want the rest of my family knowing any details—I felt way too embarrassed about what I had done. Besides, they would not have understood why I did it. So, I decided that when I told Linda about it, I would just refer to it as "The Contest". Linda would surely take the cue and then I would not have to explain.

I could not wait to see the look of excitement on her face when she found out she had won.

At six o'clock that evening, my family of five sat down at the table for dinner. As usual, everyone discussed the goings-on of their day.

I waited until everyone had finished talking. Then I turned to Linda and announced proudly and enthusiastically, "Your teacher called today. He told me I did a really good job and that you definitely won the contest!"

Linda asked, "What teacher?"

"You know…" I answered, believing that she actually did know but had momentarily forgotten. "He called about the contest."

She looked puzzled. "What contest?"

Trying to be discreet, I pressed on. "You know. The *contest*…?"

"No, I *don't* know! What are you *talking* about?" She looked visibly annoyed with me.

It frustrated me that she would not take the cue. I did not want to explain to my entire family that I had participated in a sex contest earlier that day. I could not imagine that news going over very well. But it seemed I had no other way to convey it to her. I did not want to wait any longer. So, I just blurted it out.

"You know—the *sex* contest!"

Acutely aware of the shock value of my words, I glanced over at my mother to see her reaction. The color rapidly drained from her face.

Linda stared at me in utter confusion and insisted, "We aren't *having* any contest."

Everyone stopped eating. All eyes focused on me. My mind flashed back to what had happened earlier that day; what I had been asked to say and do. Suddenly, my whole being felt contaminated.

My mother shouted, "Oh my God! I'm calling the police!"

What I had just divulged had clearly shocked and upset her and she did not know what to do about it. But considering the incident had occurred several hours ago, it seemed pointless to make an emergency call to the police. I did not understand how they could possibly help the situation.

At ten years old, I had just had a traumatic sexual experience; one I did not know how to process. I felt overcome with humiliation and self-blame. I needed reassurance and comfort. I needed understanding and support. I needed someone to tell me I had done nothing wrong. I did not need a total stranger asking me questions about my humiliating experience.

But it seemed the need for my mother to report the crime took precedence over my emotional state, which, by the way, no one ever addressed.

The police never caught the pervert, not that I expected them to. In fact, we never heard another word about it.

Someone stole my innocence that day and no one would take responsibility for it.

No worries. I could handle it. I buried the unresolved emotions about the sexual violation somewhere deep inside as I did with all my feelings, and then shored my emotions up for the next inevitable crisis.

My badly traumatized mother never spoke of the incident again.

The Homework Assignment

....

The cardinal virtue of a teacher is to protect the pupil from his own influence. ~Ralph Waldo Emerson

....

I began sixth grade in 1969 at eleven years old. My class made history as the first sixth grade to ever attend the school. It had changed from a junior high school to a middle school, a new concept in our county school system.

Since I had academically excelled throughout Elementary School, they placed me in all accelerated level classes for sixth grade.

I cannot recall the names of many of my teachers that year, but I never forgot the name of one of them—my English teacher, Mr. Faulkner.

In appearance, speech, and demeanor, Mr. Faulkner had the traits typically associated with a literary professor. He challenged his students to stretch their minds and elicited great respect from them.

My memories of Mr. Faulkner had nothing to do with his teaching style, but rather an incident that lingered with me for years.

One day while all the students in my class worked independently, Mr. Faulkner called me over to his desk. I felt honored to be singled out; for what I did not know.

I approached his desk from the front, but he motioned for me to come around and stand beside him. Then, in a quiet voice, he asked me, "Do you know how sultry you are?" Mr. Faulkner randomly challenged his students with vocabulary words, so his question did not seem out of the ordinary.

I told him I had never heard that word before and did not know how to answer his question.

He explained that he did not expect me to know the meaning of the word, but that he did want me to learn it and stretch my vocabulary. He offered to give me extra credit to do so.

He wrote the word "sultry" at the top of a piece of loose-leaf paper and handed it to me. He suggested I turn it in the next day.

The challenge intrigued me. I wondered what the mystery word meant and how it related to the question he had posed. When I got home from school that afternoon, I went right to the dictionary.

Words listed in the dictionary often have multiple meanings as did the word "sultry". The first entry defined "sultry" as "oppressively hot and moist". I did not understand the definition in the context Mr. Faulkner had used it and could not imagine what "hot and moist" had to do with me.

Assuming that definition pretty well summed up all of them, I looked no further. I copied "oppressively hot and moist" onto the paper he gave me and closed the dictionary.

Just before English class the following day, I approached Mr. Faulkner at his desk. As I handed him my paper, I pointed out that I had looked up the word sultry in the dictionary, but did not know if I had gotten the definition right because the meaning made no sense to me.

He read what I had written on the paper, then looked up at me, smiled, and replied, "The word sultry also means sexy."

I stood there blankly staring at him. A creepy tingly feeling started in my groin and rushed up to my throat. It was the same nauseating sensation I had experienced around men as a young child.

I had no idea how to respond to his immodest revelation. "Thank you" did not seem appropriate. But I could think of nothing else. So,

I forced an uncomfortable smile, thanked him for the compliment, and walked to my desk.

I sat at my desk for the rest of the period replaying the scene. It concerned me that I may have somehow solicited Mr. Faulkner's attraction. If, in fact, I *was* sending out sexual signals, I wanted to stop doing it.

Mr. Faulkner did not approach me again that way and I never told anyone about the incident. For one, I felt responsible for it, and two, it did not seem serious enough to upset my mother over. She could have done nothing about it anyway.

For the rest of the school year, every time I entered that classroom, that same creepy, nauseating feeling overtook me. Unable to focus in class, my grades began to drop.

Misguided by naïve, false assumptions, I began feeling acutely self-conscious around strange grown men. It seemed as if wherever I went, they all had eyes on me.

As it turned out, some did.

Never Talk to Strangers

....

If you let a person talk long enough, you'll hear their true intentions. Listen twice, speak once. ~Tupac Shakur

....

My grandparents lived in a brick row house in the city, just on the outskirts of the county line in a quiet, safe, predominantly Jewish neighborhood. As a child, I often slept over their house on the weekends.

They lived only three blocks from the biggest shopping center in that area, The Reisterstown Road Plaza.

"The Plaza" as everyone called it, was an open-air complex anchored by two department stores and lined with a variety of other stores.

As the social hub of that area, senior citizens living in nearby neighborhoods often met there in the afternoons, congregating at tables or benches in the center of the plaza. Teenagers often spent their Saturdays hanging out there and shopping with friends.

After turning twelve, my grandparents allowed me to take the short walk from their house to The Plaza alone. I felt very independent and mature with that freedom.

My parents had drilled the usual lectures about not talking to strangers into my head. A girl my age had recently been abducted and murdered not far from there, so I knew to stay tuned in and remain wary.

One Saturday afternoon at The Plaza, as I stood inside a store looking through stacks of blue jeans on a shelf, a man, nice looking and well-dressed, approached me. Knowing that looks can be deceiving, I ignored him when he began speaking to me.

Using my slight to his advantage, he commented that I *should* ignore strangers. I should *never* talk to people I don't know. But he stressed that I did not have to be afraid of him because he was a Baltimore County police detective.

Due to my age, he must have assumed I would buy the "don't talk to strangers, trust police officers" ruse. I did not. I turned my head away and continued ignoring him. He kept talking.

He claimed that the reason he had dressed in plain clothes instead of his uniform was that he was on an undercover assignment.

I did not believe his claim and kept ignoring him. He continued talking.

He asked me to please not tell anyone about him because he did not want his "cover" blown.

I did not plan to tell anyone, not because "it would blow his cover", but because the challenge intrigued me. I saw it as a way to test my resiliency.

The man claimed he had something very important to tell me. He said I did not need to turn around or respond, but asked me to please listen.

I didn't want to listen. I just wanted him to shut up and leave me alone.

Feeling confined by his invasion of my personal space and claustrophobic standing at that wall, I decided to relocate myself. I walked over to a round rack of clothing, hoping it would shake him loose.

The jerk followed right behind me and stood next to me, sidling up so close I felt his breath on my ear when he whispered to me.

Repulsed, I yanked myself away, looked him right in the eyes, and emphatically told him to get away from me.

He pleaded with me to just give him one minute of my time. He promised if I still wanted him to leave me alone after I heard him out, he would go away.

Hoping to extricate myself with a different strategy, I told him he had exactly one minute to say whatever he wanted to say to me. I looked down at my watch and defiantly stood there watching the time as he weaved his incredulous story.

> He told me that he and his two partners were staging a drug bust outside the store and needed a civilian decoy to distract their target. After observing me for a while, he thought I seemed very mature for my age and that I would be perfect for the mission. The drug dealer would never suspect that a child was involved. I would be in no danger whatsoever.

I might have been young but definitely not stupid. No one in their right mind would have bought such a ridiculous story. The mere fact that he thought I would believe him angered me.

I looked at him sternly and told him to stop harassing me or I would report him.

He begged me to hear him out. He agreed that the story sounded bizarre and totally understood why I did not believe any of it, but asked for one more minute of my time. He promised he could prove his allegation.

I stipulated that he had one minute, no more.

He asked me to follow him to the front of the store, and then stand in front of the window.

He opened the door and went outside. I watched as he discreetly pointed to two plain-clothed men standing across the plaza. Both men, just as discreetly, nodded back at him.

He looked at me through the glass door as if to say, "Now do you believe me?"

I have to admit, there seemed to be a kernel of truth to his story but not enough for me to trust him.

I shook my head no.

He came back inside the store, looked at me with pleading eyes, and asked me to please reconsider. "Why don't you want to help us get a very dangerous man off the streets?"

I told him to stop pressuring me. Nothing he could do or say would change my mind.

The man finally relented. He respectfully acknowledged the position I had taken and expressed his appreciation for the time I had given him. He asked how he could repay me.

I told him he did not have to do that.

Unwilling to take no for an answer, he asked, "Can I at least buy you a fountain Coke at the drugstore?"

I told him, "No, thank you."

He accused me of being unfair and tried to lay guilt on me for not allowing him to do something nice for me.

He made me feel a little guilty about turning him down, and slightly sorry for distrusting him. He seemed like a nice man. I wondered if I had misjudged him.

I took a few seconds to consider the logistics of going to the drugstore with him and weighing the risks.

I figured with so many people at The Plaza, we would be highly visible. Why would a potential kidnapper want to parade his victim around like that? And most importantly, we did not have to leave the confines of The Plaza to walk there. All things considered, I saw no foreseeable risk.

I agreed to go with him but made it clear that under no circumstances would I leave the shopping center with him.

He swore he had no reason to ask me to.

We arrived at the drugstore together without incident and then went back to the lunch counter. We sat down next to each other on the black padded chrome stools stationed there and he ordered two fountain Cokes.

As we sipped our Cokes, he talked, I listened. Knowing the "repaying me with a Coke" idea could be part of his nefarious scheme, I paid very close attention to his words, screening them for clues.

He told me all about his job as a police detective. Then he started talking about his police car. He asked if I had ever been inside one.

I told him I had not.

He mentioned that he had parked his police car in the lot behind the drugstore and offered to show it to me, if I had any interest.

While en route to the drugstore, he promised he had no reason to ask me to go outside with him. Now he had asked me to do just that. I knew he was trying to lure me out there.

I had heard enough.

I looked down at my watch and exclaimed, "Oh no. I didn't realize the time. My mother is going to be upset with me for not calling when I promised I would. I've got to go. She's going to be worried."

Then I reached into my purse, pulled out a dime, and excused myself to use the payphone.

Outsmarted by a twelve-year-old girl, he paid the check, thanked me for my time, and then stood up and walked out the back door.

Longing for the safety of my grandparents' house, I left the store and dashed through the shopping center. Then I ran as fast as I could to their house.

I did not want to upset my grandparents or parents by telling them what had happened to me. Worrying them meant losing my freedom.

I took pride in the fact that I had faced a dangerous situation and come out of it victorious.

I stood outside my grandparents' house until I caught my breath, composed myself, and then walked into their house as if nothing had happened.

Too Hideous to Love

....

A poor self-image is the magnifying glass that can transform a trivial mistake or imperfection into an overwhelming symbol of personal defeat. ~David D. Burns

....

When I think of my childhood years, those three episodes, all involving adult men, stand out clearest in my mind. Though I remained physically unscathed, experience continued to shape my belief that my ability to please and my appearance were all that mattered. I got lots of attention, often inappropriate, for my exterior, but no one seemed to value me as a person.

Depressive moods often overtook me. I would try to share how I felt with my mother and she would always say, "Why are you depressed? You have nothing to be unhappy about, you're beautiful!"

Her words continually affirmed that my feelings did not matter, my personality did not matter; only my looks and ability to please mattered.

My subconscious mind amalgamated those beliefs into one personal truth; no one would love or value an imperfect Randi.

Without a healthy emotional foundation on which to build my

life and a poor self-image, I entered my fragile teenage years entirely unprepared for the emotional roller-coaster ride that lie ahead.

My guitar had been a constant companion ever since I had learned to play it at six years old. I used to spend hours alone in my room each day playing it, singing, and writing songs. It went everywhere I went. My friends always wanted me to entertain them. They used to tell me I would be famous one day.

When I played music, I felt transported out of the reality of my life into a higher, more peaceful realm. Music nurtured my soul in a way nothing else could.

My love of music drew me to other kids with the same interest. At the beginning of tenth grade, I met some talented kids who went to the same high school I did and we decided to form a band.

I sang lead vocals with another girl, played some acoustic guitar, and wrote songs for the band. We took our music very seriously and accomplished a lot for our age.

My bandmates were like family to me. It did not matter if we played music or just hung out, we just really liked spending time together.

Our practice house was my home away from home. I never wanted to leave the emotional safe haven, the place where I could feel peaceful. I dreaded going back to the chaos of my own home.

My bandmates were not my only friends. I had a best girlfriend and a large group of friends I had known since elementary and middle school.

One Saturday night, in the spring of my fifteenth year, my friends and I got together at one of their houses.

One of the girls had her driver's license and had borrowed her father's car for the night. She wanted to go to McDonald's to get some food and asked if anyone wanted to go with her. My best friend and I volunteered.

I had fallen pretty hard for a guy at my High School that liked me too, but for some reason, would not commit to a relationship with me. When we were together, I felt on top of the world. More often than not, I felt deeply depressed over him.

I did not expect to see him at McDonald's that night but it definitely made me happy when I walked in and saw him there, sitting at a table.

My two friends and I walked over to his table to say hello. The girl who had driven us plopped right down beside him and the two of them began flagrantly flirting with each other in front of me. It devastated me to watch him coming on to another girl, so much so it ruined my entire night.

From that moment on, I just wanted to go home, get in bed, and cry my eyes out.

I told my best friend that we needed to leave. She totally understood why. We obviously could not ask the girl who drove us there to get off the lap of the guy I liked and take us home.

My girlfriend noticed a couple of older guys from our school hanging out there. She knew them through her older brother, but I did not know any of them. She asked if someone would be willing to give us a ride home and one of the guys agreed to.

It just so happened that the guy who offered to drive us home lived across the street from the house where our band practiced. He knew me. I did not know him.

My girlfriend lived closer to McDonald's than I did, so he dropped her off at her house first. Then I gave him directions to my neighborhood.

When we got to the top of the street I lived on, I asked him to drop me off there. I did not want to risk having my parents see me get out of a strange boy's car.

He offered to take me directly to my house but I told him I wanted to walk home from there. I thanked him for the ride and got out of the car.

When I closed the car door, I accidentally slammed my left index finger in it. I felt the sensation of the impact but did not realize how seriously I had hurt myself—until I looked at it. When

I did, I saw that I had lost the top half-inch of my finger. Blood was hemorrhaging heavily out of the gaping wound. It looked like a scene out of a horror movie.

Terrified at the sight of my injury, I let out a long chain of blood-curdling screams. People living on that street poured out of their houses to see what had happened.

Hearing my screams, the driver jumped out of his car. When he saw my injury, he told me not to worry—he had paramedic training and knew exactly what to do.

He sprung right into action. He opened his trunk, grabbed a towel, and tightly wrapped my finger in it to slow down the bleeding. Then he ushered me into the front seat of his car, put his emergency flashing lights on, and sped to the nearest hospital emergency room.

As we drove there, I remember asking him if my finger would grow back and him telling me it would. I'm sure he knew it would not but wanted to keep me as calm as possible.

We arrived at the hospital emergency room in minutes. The emergency room staff took it from there.

I thanked him for all he had done for me and told him he could go home. I assured him that I would be okay, even though I knew I would not be. I was in shock and terrified, but I did not want to waste any more of the guy's time. Someone who less than an hour ago had been a stranger to me had gone above and beyond to help me in my desperate time of need.

The hospital staff tried over and over to reach my parents but could not. They had yet to come home from their night out.

An hour or so later, when they did arrive home, they walked in to the sound of the telephone ringing. Unfortunately, it was my mother not my father who picked up the phone to answer the call. When she heard what had happened to me, she physically went into shock.

My father, always invaluable in a crisis, already had one foot out the door, ready to go to the hospital. My mother stood frozen by the telephone and would not move. He had to yank her by the hand, physically pull her out of the house, and shove her into the car.

By the time the hospital had reached my parents, I had gone through surgery alone. Fully bandaged, I waited alone in a room for my parents to get there so the hospital could discharge me.

Only fifteen years old, I had gone through the most terrifying crisis of my life with no loved ones by my side. I cannot fault my parents for not being there. Mobile phones had yet to exist. How could they have possibly known what had happened to me?

The hospital staff and the doctor had treated me wonderfully but they had a job to do. No one held my hand or comforted me.

After the McDonald's incident, I just wanted to go home, get in bed, and cry my eyes out. Hours later, I still had not gotten there. And now, in addition to my broken heart and depression, I was exhausted, in pain, and completely traumatized.

When I saw my parents walk in the room, I felt a huge relief. My father knew exactly what to say to comfort me. My mother, clearly a total wreck, tried her best to do the same. After seeing her in such a frazzled state, I became more concerned for her than for myself.

The ordeal kept me in bed and out of commission for the next two weeks. Though the doctor prescribed potent narcotics for the unrelenting, excruciating pain, nothing helped. Grieving and traumatized over what had happened to me, I could not get out of bed.

I could hardly bear the emotional torment I felt. I beat myself up over and over for having made such a stupid mistake that left me permanently defective, deformed, and too hideous to love. Forever scarred and imperfect, I believed I had nothing left to live for.

After a few weeks, the wound healed enough that I no longer needed a bandage. But I had yet to look at my finger and still refused to. I could not face the reality of my injury. I insisted the doctor put another bandage on and cover it back up.

The bandage stayed on for a few more weeks while I tried to muster up the courage to face the reality of my injury.

One afternoon, while in the middle of Social Studies class, a surge of courage rose up inside me. I told my teacher I did not feel well and asked to go to the school nurse.

I explained my fear of facing my injury to the nurse and asked her to help me take the bandage off.

Thanks to her great compassion and support, I finally faced the visual reality of my injury. I still had not emotionally come to terms with what had happened to me. No one talked about PTSD in those years, but in retrospect, I know that I definitely had it.

Hopeful I could still play my guitar, the faithful friend always there to soothe and console me, I made a few attempts.

Unfortunately, it caused me physical pain every time I tried. Grievously discouraged, I gave up. It seemed I had lost everything.

The entire trauma knocked me into a black hole of depression I could not pull myself out of. Nothing anyone could say or do would make me feel better—I remained inconsolable. My injury had rendered me damaged goods. No one would ever love me again.

My mother, who did a wonderful job of catering to my physical needs during my first two weeks in bed, could not begin to deal with my challenging emotional state. She asked me if I wanted to see a psychologist to get some help, but I could not bear to relive what had happened and refused to go.

One afternoon, a deep, mournful crying jag took me over (as they often did). Still devastated by what had happened to me and completely unable to cope with the reality of it, I needed encouraging words and compassion. I desperately needed a new perspective; a hopeful one that would put the light back in my life.

My mother, the only family member home at the time, heard me crying and came into the room. Her words to me were: "Randi—you just lost a little piece of your finger. When are you going to stop all this crying? …Enough already!"

Her harsh words only made me feel worse and cry harder.

In total exasperation, she shouted, "Randi, I can't take it from you anymore. I'm going out." And that's exactly what she did. She left me all alone in a state of deep, inconsolable despair because *she* couldn't deal with it.

When I reminded her of that incident years later, she responded, and I quote, "How can you say I didn't care? I lost sleep over it every night."

I do not know how my mother losing sleep benefitted me in any way. And I don't know how long it took her to recover or if she ever did, but it took me well over two decades.

Booby-Trapped

....

*How stupid that all I have to do is grow two
squishy lumps and suddenly I'm man's best friend.*
~Christine Heppermann, Poisoned Apples

....

My first two years of high school were not happy ones. I spent most of them in deep depression. I had decent grades but had not applied myself academically. Once I reached my senior year, I wanted to have as little to do with the school as possible. I just wanted out of there.

I enrolled in a senior program called Diversified Occupation, an alternative to a full day at school. I only had to take English and a D.O. class every morning, and then work at a paying job outside of the school for the remainder of the day. Enough credits were earned through that program to graduate at the end of the year.

At the beginning of the school year, I began working at the office of a company that billed patients for doctor visits.

Three men, all related, owned the company. Two of the partners were Filipino brothers, both married. The third partner, their American brother-in-law, was married to their sister.

The brothers never called me Randi. They just called me "Boobs".

With their accent, it sounded more like *Bull-bs* (like a male cow with a bs at the end).

At the time, I did not think of myself as naïve, but I must have been. I never corrected them or told them to stop. The pet-name seemed harmless.

One afternoon, after having worked in the office for about three months, the brothers called downstairs and asked me to come up to their private office. I worked in the downstairs office with another lady and had never been asked to go up there before. I could not imagine what they wanted from me.

I rode the elevator up to the second floor and located their office. Then I knocked on the door and heard a familiar voice with a Filipino accent on the other side say, "Come on in, Boobs. The door is unlocked."

I opened the door and saw the two brothers casually swiveling back and forth in their desk chairs, looking at me with stupid smiles on their faces.

"Come in, don't be shy," they remarked, practically in unison. I walked in and closed the door behind me.

They both stood up and guided me towards an adjacent room with a wide opening and no door.

I first saw the long, yellow upholstered bench against the back wall. As I made my way into the room, I noticed a large chrome and glass étagère on the left side, neatly stacked with several piles of magazines.

One of the brothers patted his hand on the yellow bench. "Sit here, Boobs."

As I reluctantly lowered myself onto the seat, I noticed the other brother removing a magazine from one of the many piles on the étagère.

He brought the magazine over to me, opened it to a specific page, and then laid it on my lap. The photograph showed a nude young girl seductively posed in a pornographic magazine.

"That girl is seventeen just like you. Is that what *you* look like, Boobs?"

Alarmed but not wanting to give them the satisfaction of seeing my reaction, I nonchalantly replied, "I don't think so."

"We think so," one of them quickly retorted, both laughing. "Why don't you take off your shirt and show us *your* boobs?"

Feeling vulnerable and nervous, but unwilling to show it, I assumed an air of arrogance. Then I abruptly retorted, "You must be kidding. I will *not* take my shirt off for you."

They tried to coerce me through intimidation. "Are you too modest? Come on, Boobs, don't be a chicken." Clearly enjoying the game, they kept the pressure on for a few minutes longer. I stood my ground.

Finally, one of them remarked to the other, "She's too chicken." Then he turned toward me with a disgusted look on his face. "We're done with you. You can go back downstairs, Boobs."

Never letting them see me sweat, I calmly walked out of their office and went back downstairs as if nothing had happened. They stayed upstairs for the rest of the day.

When I showed up for work the next morning, the other lady I worked with passed the message on to me that the brothers had fired me.

The despicable behavior of my bosses did not shock me. I had come to expect that sort of conduct from grown men.

Still, I felt responsible for what happened to me. Somehow, I must have sent the wrong message—once again.

No one, neither my teacher nor my parents would know the circumstances behind the firing unless I told them.

I concocted a story that everyone bought and then added the degrading experience to my emotional crap pile.

> It never occurred to me to report those men for "sexual harassment." At the time of my firing, sexual harassment was not recognized as a crime. The very first sexual harassment court decision in America did, in fact, happen that same year, 1976, but the term did not become a household word until 1991 when Paula Jones filed a lawsuit against President Bill Clinton for it.

Off the Wall

....

Being an artist means forever healing your own wounds and at the same time endlessly exposing them. ~Annette Messager

....

I graduated high school in June of 1976 during the bicentennial anniversary of our country. Tall, majestic sailing ships from all over the world docked at the Baltimore harbor that summer. Thousands of tourists flooded the city each day.

I planned to start my freshman year of college in August of that year at a local university.

I chose to live at home, primarily because I did not want to leave my boyfriend. I also stayed around because I felt guilty about abandoning my mother even though she would not have been alone. She had my father. But she always insisted that she did not know what she would do without me.

My older siblings had already relocated to other states and whether intentional or not, left me with the entire burden of trying to keep my mother happy.

I excitedly began the fall semester of college with two majors, Art and Psychology. I planned to eventually merge the two majors into one and graduate as an Art Therapist.

Before long, it became crystal clear that I had made a very bad decision not going away to college. My boyfriend and I broke up soon after the semester started, and my home life had gone from very bad to calamitous.

I liked school—at least some of it. I really enjoyed my art and psychology classes. I fully applied myself in those courses and got excellent grades. But my lack of focus in high school proved to be detrimental to my success in other subjects.

I never developed good study habits and had no language arts skills to speak of. I barely eked by in my freshman prerequisite courses. But I persevered and managed to make it through my freshman year.

I had similar issues with general studies courses in the first semester of my sophomore year. I despised English Literature and ultimately failed that class. I also found it frustrating how much home time I had to devote to my art assignments. At eighteen, I wanted to be careless, wild, and crazy—not saddled down with hours of homework.

During the second semester of my sophomore year, I took a sculpting class, an art major requirement. The greatest percentage of the final grade for the semester came from the completion of a wood sculpture.

I came up with an original idea, sketched out a plan for an abstract wall sculpture, and once I got approval on it, approached the challenge with great enthusiasm.

The sculpture was an interesting three-dimensional study of depth and shading. I used an intricate, time-consuming technique that took over a hundred hours to complete. The hard work paid off. The piece came out beautifully.

I completed the project just before spring break. My instructor, very impressed with my work, asked if I would mind loaning it to him over Spring break. He wanted to display it in the Fine Arts Building.

Though anxious to bring it home, I felt honored that he liked it so much. I assumed he planned to hang it in the art gallery on the first floor of the Fine Arts Building. Knowing it would be safe in there under lock and key, I agreed to loan it to him.

The first day back to school after break, I went to the art gallery, anxious to see my sculpture displayed among the other exceptional student works of art.

I looked around the entire gallery but did not see my sculpture hanging anywhere. My instructor never actually told me where he would hang it. I had made that assumption, obviously the wrong one, entirely on my own.

Figuring he must have put it in a locked glass display case, I walked every floor of the Fine Arts building looking for it but could not locate it anywhere. Confused and panicky, I went looking for my teacher. I hoped that nothing had happened to it.

I found him in the sculpture studio and asked him about it.

To my horror, he explained how he hung my sculpture on a nail on the wall in the hallway across from the studio right before break, and found it missing when he returned.

My heart sank. I stared at him in disbelief.

In a failed attempt to add levity to the upset he caused, he suggested I take it as a compliment that someone liked my sculpture enough to steal it. He did apologize for what had happened, but not for what he had done.

His apology and consolation did not make up for his negligence and stupidity. How could the moron have hung it on a nail on the wall? Of course someone would steal it.

Hoping that someone at school knew its whereabouts, I placed an ad in the university newspaper and posted signs all around campus. No one responded. My prized piece was forever gone.

My whole being felt dejected. The sculpture represented my emergence of self, the forming of a separate and distinct identity, and the long-overdue validation of my personal excellence. I deeply grieved the loss of it.

I had always bared my heart and soul through music and art. No walls existed between me and them. I had already lost the ability to play guitar. Now this happened.

Years of unresolved depression and grief came bursting through the dam I had built to hold those emotions back.

Just as my sculpture had vanished, so did my enthusiasm for school. After completing my sophomore year of college, I dropped out.

My home life had become unbearable; my parents downright hostile. As a young adult no longer wishing to conform to the confusing rigidity of their expectations, I had become the enemy.

They despised my new boyfriend, Greg. The things they hated about him were the exact traits that had drawn me to him to begin with: he was not Jewish and he had a smart-aleck attitude.

Try as they might, their hostile attempts to dissuade the relationship only backfired. The more they pushed to keep me away from him, the further they drove me into his arms.

My parents were disgusted with my attitude and disagreed with my choices. I'd had my fill of their redundant lectures and histrionic reactions.

I could no longer live in the middle of a war zone. Rebellion boiled inside of me, then shot out like steam from a tea kettle. I had to get out of there before I went insane and/or my parents and I killed each other.

To Sir with Angst

....

People with high ego and unnecessary attitude deserve the standing ovation of the tallest finger. ~Shahrukh Malik Noida

....

After dropping out of college, I got a job working full-time for a premium finance company. The job did not pay well but at least I had an income.

In order to get out of my parents' house and live on my own, I had to find a roommate to share expenses with. I began combing the classifieds.

I met with a few nice people, but something about them or their living arrangements did not click with me. I felt very discouraged. Then I found a promising ad in the *Jewish Times* that read: A female living in a two-bedroom, two-bath apartment in Randallstown is looking for another female to share expenses with. I had a good feeling about that one.

My hunch was right. The instant I met Sandra, the young woman who had placed the ad, our personalities clicked. She had a clean, spacious apartment, I liked the location, and best of all, I could afford it. We agreed to be roommates.

I could not wait to break free from the prison I had spent the last nineteen years living in. I moved in with Sandra a few days later.

I had never felt such a joyous, liberating feeling.

I did not mind working to pay for my freedom. I only wished I made more money. My modest salary did not leave me much spending money after all the bills were paid.

If Sandra had been struggling right along with me, it probably would not have bothered me as much. But she was not. The contrast between our situations made mine seem that much worse.

She had a professional college degree and earned nearly twice the salary I did. She had money to buy a new car, travel—do pretty much whatever she wanted to do. I lived a no-frills life.

I struggled for two years to make ends meet before deciding to look for a better job.

With no college degree and no plans to return to school, I knew a well-paying job would be hard to find. But I thought if I could possibly find a professional job that offered marketable skill-training and growth, then the initial low salaried trade-off would be worth it.

I saw an ad in the Sunday classifieds that sparked my interest. An unspecified law firm was seeking an office clerk. The position included paralegal training. It could not have sounded more perfect for me.

I cut out the ad and called first thing Monday morning, hoping to set up an interview. Fortunately, they still had the position open and they scheduled a time for me to come in.

The lady who arranged the interview advised me I would be meeting with the president of the firm. After she disclosed the name and address of the firm, I did some research.

I learned that the man I would be meeting with, the president of the firm, was a well-known malpractice attorney famous for having won several high-profile, multi-million dollar cases. If everything worked out, I could have the opportunity of a lifetime.

On the day of the interview, determined to make a great impression, I walked into his office brimming with confidence. I extended my hand before he did and gave him a firm handshake. Then I turned on the charm.

The interview went well. He seemed easy to talk to and I could tell he liked me. At the end of the interview, he offered me the job. I could not believe my luck. This job would completely turn my life around. The next morning, I gave a two-week notice at my job.

On the first day of my job at the firm, as per his instructions, I arrived early and reported directly to the executive secretary. Strangely, no one had informed her of my hire so she had no idea what to do with me. The president, in court all day, could not be reached.

She seated me at an empty desk in the waiting area and told me to read magazines until further notice.

The next day, the same exact thing happened. I arrived for work bright and early in the morning and reported to the executive secretary. Still unprepared for me, she told me to sit at the same desk I had sat at the day before and read magazines.

She wanted me to also answer the phone. As per her instructions, answering the phone just meant taking messages. She told me never to put a call through to any of the attorneys.

The secretary advised me that everyone at the law firm addressed the president as "Sir" and that I should do the same. I thought it seemed very egotistical.

I asked if I could do anything to help her while I sat there, but she said no. Just answer the phones and continue reading magazines—until further notice.

I came to work the next two mornings hoping for a better outcome, only to be told the same thing; read magazines and answer the telephone—until further notice.

After the longest, most boring four days of my life, I approached the secretary to ask if she knew when my training would begin. Annoyed that I dared to question her, she arrogantly suggested I be patient.

At "Sir's" mercy, just like everyone else at the firm, I could do nothing to remedy the preposterous situation.

Finally, on Friday morning, the secretary advised me that my training would begin on Monday. I looked forward to getting started. I hoped to never see another magazine again.

On Monday morning, I reported to the executive secretary. She told me to get my coat; we were going on an errand.

I put on my coat, followed her out into the hall, and we took an elevator down to the basement garage. She pointed to a fleet of cars while explaining, in her dry impersonal manner, that we had to go pick up "Sir's" weekly wholesale produce order.

She handed me a legal pad and pen and recommended I take notes since I would eventually assume that responsibility.

The secretary drove the company station wagon while I rode next to her, writing down the directions on my legal pad.

An hour later, we arrived at the wholesale produce market.

She parked the station wagon in a specific spot, got out of the car, and waited until one of the workers attended to her.

The worker then went inside the warehouse, came out wheeling a tall stack of boxes on a hand-truck, stacked them beside the car, and then went back inside to get more.

I watched the secretary inspect each box for accuracy and freshness. She reminded me to take notes so I would know how to do it myself.

After the two of us loaded all the boxes into the back of the company station wagon, we headed back to Baltimore. I thought we would go back to the office but I soon discovered we had more errands to run.

I certainly did not expect to be used as a gopher on my first day of paralegal training or be told I would eventually have to take that job over. It all seemed so bizarre.

I had no idea what she expected me to write other than noting the directions to and from the market. There was nothing complicated or mentally challenging about the experience. But with her watching every move I made, I pretended to take notes.

On the way back, she told me we had a few more errands to run. Our next stop would be at the Dry Cleaners to pick up "Sir's" clothes. Then we had to go to his house to drop off his dry cleaning and all the produce.

The secretary backed the station wagon halfway into his garage and together we unloaded the boxes of produce from the back. She told me to stack them neatly against the wall. As I did that, she went inside the house to put his dry cleaning away.

When all tasks were completed, she drove us back downtown to the office, parking the station wagon in the exact same spot as before.

The next morning, I arrived for work and experienced Groundhog Day all over again. I spent the next four days reading magazines and being ignored. It seemed as if they were trying to humiliate me or break me down for some reason. It worked. I felt like a worthless peasant.

I arrived for work on the Monday morning of my third week expecting to have another mind-numbing day. As usual, I reported to the executive secretary.

She advised me that "Sir" would like to see me in his office. She instructed me to wait at my desk until he called for me.

About fifteen minutes later, she notified me through the intercom on my desk phone that "Sir" would see me now. The door to his office swung open and he cordially invited me in.

"Sir" began our meeting, apologizing for ignoring me for the last few weeks. He explained that he had given a lot of thought to where he wanted to place me and that he had now come up with a proposal.

That puzzled me. I thought the responsibilities of my job had been defined the day he hired me.

He began by stressing that the position he had in mind for me "carried great responsibility."

He went on to explain that I would be his "right-hand" assistant.

He would expect me to be accessible to him 24/7, day and night through the beeper he would provide for me.

After he finished elaborating on his proposal, he maintained that if I preferred, I could still have the job I had been hired for.

Though tempted by the substantial increase in salary associated with the great responsibility, I did not want to be controlled and manipulated by him as it appeared others in the office had been. I had only been there a few weeks and could already see how he turned employees into his self-serving robots.

And the fact that he wanted full access to me at all times seemed very suspicious. Every instinct I had told me not to accept that position.

But above all, I tremendously valued my personal space and freedom. I had worked too hard and sacrificed too much to have those things. I did not want him or anyone else interrupting my private life at whim.

I thanked him for the wonderful opportunity and told him I felt more comfortable staying with the job he had originally hired me for.

The offer had been presented to me unconditionally, or so it seemed, and he appeared to have no problem with my decision. I left "Sir's" office on very friendly terms.

The next morning, I arrived at work ready to start my training. As usual, I checked in with the secretary. She told me to wait at my desk for instructions.

A few minutes after I sat down, a partner of the firm I had yet to meet approached me, introduced himself, and asked me to come into his office. I assumed he had work to give me or something to teach me.

He offered me a seat in his office and then closed the door behind him.

He sat down at his desk facing me, looked directly at me, and then slightly dropped his eyes.

"You're fired," he said as gently as possible.

My jaw dropped. "I haven't even started the job yet! Why am I being fired? What did I do wrong?"

Nodding at me in a knowing way, he replied, "You chose the wrong job."

That bastard "Sir" had set me up.

> Seven years later, two FBI agents visited me at my job. They verified that I had worked for that particular law firm in 1979 and asked me why I had left. I explained the strange circumstances of my firing. They disclosed that a few other women, all blonde and physically resembling me, had experienced the same treatment I had. One of them reported it. They now had "Sir" under federal investigation for repeated sexual harassment in the workplace. I don't know if he ever got convicted of the crime but found great satisfaction in just knowing he might be charged.

A Living Nightmare

....

Man is the only predator who hunts his own. ~Kenneth Eade, Unwanted

....

Jobless through no fault of my own, I filed for unemployment to help pay my living expenses until I could find another job.

After a few months, I landed a job as the credit manager for a popular jewelry store conveniently located at the Reisterstown Road Plaza.

I had a lot of freedom with that position. With the exception of occasional visits from the regional supervisor, who I got along very well with, I had no boss.

While commuting to work one morning, I accidentally rear-ended the car in front of me that had stopped at a traffic light. I had not been going very fast and, thankfully, no one got hurt.

The back of the car I hit barely showed a scratch. My car did not fare nearly as well. The hood folded up like a crushed soda can.

Due to the age of my car, the insurance company deemed it a total loss.

Fortunately, my parents came through for me. They were about to buy a new car and offered to give me their old one. They really saved me as I could not have afforded to buy another car.

I received an insurance settlement check in the amount of two thousand dollars—not a windfall, but since I did not have to spend it on another car, I could put it in the bank for an emergency. I couldn't have possibly accumulated the financial cushion on my own.

Sandra and I had been roommates for over two years. We enjoyed sharing the apartment together and had become close friends.

She had recently started dating a really nice guy named Bob, who lived on the first floor of our apartment building. We lived on the second floor.

Bob had his own contracting company and seemed very stable. As their relationship grew more serious, she began spending more time with him and she often slept over at his apartment.

My boyfriend Greg and I had been together for two drama-filled, tumultuous years. Since the moment I met him, his life had been chronically problematic. A laundry list of troubles, legal and otherwise, constantly followed him.

Though we had a frustrating and arduous relationship, Greg's brilliant mind and charismatic personality held me captive. I found him curiously interesting, mysterious, and deeply pensive.

Greg wrote beautiful poetry—mostly for or about me.

I saw great potential in him and could never understand why he continued making such bad choices. The more problems he created for himself, the harder I tried to mold him into the person I thought he could be. I refused to give up on him.

I spun my wheels trying. Greg, a dyed-in-the-wool con man had long since mastered the art of lying and cheating. I could not keep up with his antics.

The last straw came when I began receiving threatening phone calls from people he had double-crossed. I finally reached my saturation point. He had to go.

I truly expected to feel better without him in my life. I looked forward to the relief the peace would bring. But that is not what happened. I felt worse. I had become a hard-core drama junkie.

I met a few nice guys and went on some dates, but none of them interested me. I found them all boring. Everything about my life seemed boring.

The lull would not last. Two months later, trouble found me.

On August 25, 1980, two weeks shy of my twenty-second birthday, I experienced a living nightmare—the kind you hear about on the news but never dream will happen to you.

Sandra spent the night downstairs with Bob, leaving me alone in the apartment. I double-checked the dead-bolt lock on the door to our apartment around 11:30 p.m. and then went to bed.

Around three o'clock in the morning, a strange combination of sounds in my bedroom woke me out of a deep sleep.

I heard my Cockatiel hissing wildly from his cage right near my bedroom door. He did that when anyone got close to him. I also heard the squishing sound the padding under my bedroom carpet made anytime someone stepped on it.

I had closed my bedroom door before going to sleep and when I opened my eyes, I could see the bathroom nightlight shining in from the hallway.

Without my glasses on, I could only see a dark shadowy figure standing by the birdcage. My heart began to pound rapidly. Someone had entered my bedroom.

Praying I knew the person, I called out, "Who's there?"

In an instant, I felt a knife at my throat. The man holding it ordered me not to move.

Pressing the knife harder against my neck, he climbed on top of my body and pinned me down.

I could feel the clammy sweat from his bare chest transferring to my skin and smelled the cherry-scented oil he reeked of. The pendant on his necklace made a rattling sound as he moved.

Trembling with fear and sobbing, I pleaded with him not to hurt me.

Agitated by my hysteria, he demanded I calm down.

Between terrified, breathless sobs, I told him I could not calm down with a knife against my throat.

To my great relief, he moved the knife away from my neck and then reached over and laid it down on my dresser. Then he asked, "Where is your mother?"

The question seemed completely out of context, and under the circumstances, very creepy. I thought it might be some kind of sexual perversion.

I told him my mother had slept somewhere else that night. That must have satisfied him because he never asked anything more about her.

Trapped and isolated, the situation looked dire. I could not run. I could not scream. I had no hope of anyone coming to save me. Somehow, I had to save myself. My mind scrambled for a strategy.

I thought I might be less of a threat to him if he knew I could never identify him after the fact.

I told him he could do whatever he came to do and I would cooperate. And I promised not to look at his face.

I grabbed my pillow and put it over my face so he would believe me.

Rendered physically helpless, I only had one survival tool at my disposal—my mind. As the mediator of my crazy family, I had spent many years reasoning with unreasonable people and calming them down.

I knew if I could connect with his conscience and gain his compassion, I could diffuse the situation, at least a little. If he had no conscience or compassion, my chances of surviving were slim to none.

I composed myself, and then, trying to size him up, began talking to him in a friendly tone. First, I thanked him for putting the knife down. Then I asked him why he had chosen me.

He admitted he had been watching me sit outside on the front steps of my apartment building, talking to my mother.

I often sat out there talking to my next-door neighbor who looked as if she could have been my mother.

He continued on to tell me that he found me very attractive and wanted to be with me, but knew that would never be possible.

I told him how flattered I felt to know he found me attractive. Then I asked him why he thought I would not have had any interest in him and why he would go to so much trouble to be with me when he could have just asked me out.

He did not respond.

I asked him how he managed to get past the deadbolt lock on the door of my apartment.

He didn't answer my question but went on to say that he had been watching me come and go, trying to figure out which apartment I lived in.

I asked again how he got past the lock.

Proud to share the ingenuity of his plan, he explained he had not come through the front door. He came in from the balcony (facing the woods behind the building).

He described how he stood on top of my downstairs neighbor's picnic table, positioned directly under my balcony, so he could reach the railing, then he hoisted his body up and over it.

Standing on the balcony, he shook the sliding glass doors until they moved off the track and opened and then walked right into my living room.

I never heard a thing.

It horrified me to know that as I naively went about my life, he had been stalking me and calculating his plan.

I feared I might be dealing with a psychopath. If I could not connect with his conscience, I could very likely end up dead. I had to quickly figure out how his mind worked and think of a way to out-psych him.

I began asking him questions about his mother. I figured if that didn't appeal to his conscience, nothing would.

I asked if he loved and respected his mother.

He replied that he loved and respected her very much.

Then I asked if he currently or ever had a girlfriend.

He claimed that he did not have a girlfriend at the time but he'd had them in the past.

I knew asking the next question could be risky but I had to gauge his reaction.

I asked how he would feel if a man violated his mother or a woman he loved the way he was violating me.

He thought for a second, then declared, "I would be enraged."

A great sense of relief washed over me. With my life in his hands, there were no guarantees. But at least I had bought myself some time.

I began to sense he had developed some compassion for me, however warped he expressed it. He assured me that as long as I cooperated with him, he would do what he came to do and then leave.

He had come to rape me and I knew he would not leave until he completed the act. But attempting to show a little compassion, he offered that he would not ejaculate inside of me. That turned out to be a lie.

I had no say in any of it. I could only hope that if I cooperated, the nightmare would soon end.

I gritted my teeth under my pillow and tried not to think about the sexual violation. Fortunately, he did not get violent or aggressive with me.

Once he finished his business, he climbed off of me and got dressed. He announced that he would be leaving, and asked me not to call for help until I heard the sound of a rock hitting my window, indicating he had escaped.

After he finally left my room, I laid there, my body shaking uncontrollably, trying to listen for the sound of a rock hitting my window. When I did not hear it, I began to worry he might still be in the apartment.

I glanced over at the alarm clock on my night table. It was four-something in the morning.

I continued listening for sounds of him milling around the

apartment, but heard none. So, I reached for the telephone receiver next to my bed to call Sandra. My hands shook so violently, I could hardly dial Bob's number.

Bob answered the phone sounding half asleep. When he heard me hysterically ranting, he woke Sandra up and handed her the receiver.

Sandra listened to my story in utter disbelief. She told me she would call 911, get dressed, and then come right upstairs to help me.

I hung up the phone and then cautiously tiptoed to the doorway of my room. I peered left and right down the hallway. Seeing no sign of him lurking around, I bolted from my bedroom to the living room to lock the sliding glass doors.

I turned to look at the front door. The deadbolt remained locked. He had left the apartment the same way he entered it.

While hurrying past the kitchen on my way to the living room, I had noticed an open drawer, so I went back to investigate. I found our cutlery drawer rummaged through and a knife missing.

I turned left out of the kitchen and walked to the end of the hallway to Sandra's bedroom.

I entered her room and what I saw chilled me to the bone.

Like a scene right out of a slasher movie, the wire to her telephone had been cut and left lying on the floor. In that instant, the entire picture came together.

After he watched me with my neighbor on the front steps and then saw the antique furniture in Sandra's bedroom, he figured I lived with my mother.

From what I could tell, he had entered Sandra's room before entering mine. If she had not slept downstairs that night, she would have likely become his first victim and the outcome might have been far more catastrophic.

Sandra came upstairs a few minutes later. When she looked around the apartment, she discovered that the living room and kitchen telephone wires had been cut as well.

It seemed my life and potentially that of Sandra's had hung by a thread. Given what could have happened, we were both extremely fortunate. I did not care if they ever caught the rapist. I had survived with my life.

Two detectives arrived minutes after Sandra did. One began dusting our apartment for fingerprints. The other asked me to show him the crime scene.

I walked him back to my bedroom. He put on gloves and carefully bagged the bed sheets and nightgown as evidence to take with him.

They took my victim's statement and then transported me by squad car to the Baltimore County Rape Crisis Center. I went through a forensic gynecological examination. The doctor used a rape kit to gather fluids and hair samples. To prevent pregnancy, they gave me a "morning after" pill.

Since DNA profiling did not exist in 1980, even with all the evidence gathered, I still had to positively identify the rapist's face. I could not do that because I never saw it.

The detectives visited me twice more at my apartment to show me mug shots but I could not help at all.

I did not care. I had survived the attack and could not have been more grateful to be alive.

> The Postface at the end of the book tells the amazing conclusion to the story thirty years later.

The Stormy Aftermath

....

Trauma creates changes you don't choose. Healing is about creating change you do choose. ~Michele Rosenthal

....

In the weeks and months following the rape, I began to realize how emotionally detached from the sexual violation I felt.

The terror of waking up to an intruder in my room and the horror of not knowing whether I would live or die had left me severely traumatized. I had been robbed of the most valuable thing I had; the safe and secure feeling of living on my own.

The vulnerability I had always felt living in my childhood home, the over-exposed feeling of being surrounded by too many windows and unsafe doors, the one I thought I left behind when I moved out, had now become actualized in the one place I least expected it to.

But the sexual violation did not bother me at all. It just seemed as if another man had objectified me and used me for his own gratification—nothing out of the ordinary there.

I never went for therapy because I did not believe I needed it. But I was not the same person after the rape as I had been before it.

I wanted Greg to know what had happened to me but did not know how to get in touch with him. I called his mother and asked

Cliffedge Road

her to pass on the message that I had an emergency. He responded quickly by telephone and then came right over to see me.

Once he got there, I did not want him to leave. The thought of sleeping alone terrified me.

He asked if I would feel more secure having a dog around to alert me while I slept. I thought I might, so the next day we went out and he bought me a Shetland sheepdog puppy. We named him Shane.

I did not consult Sandra first, but since she had often talked about getting a dog, I did not think she would have a problem with it.

As puppies typically do, he chewed on everything and, not yet paper trained, peed everywhere. The entire apartment began to reek of urine.

It infuriated Sandra to have the apartment she took so much pride in being destroyed by a dog.

The tension between us grew more and more unbearable by the day. I took no ownership of the problems and blamed her.

I became impossible to live with. My compassionate, kind, compromising nature yielded to a hard-headed, belligerent, selfish one. The great friendship Sandra and I had built rapidly deteriorated. We could not see eye to eye on anything.

One day after she left for work, I packed up my things, took my puppy, and with Greg's help, moved out of the apartment. I left her a check to cover my portion of the rent and utilities. She had no recourse against me for future expenses because the bills were solely in her name.

Sandra had done nothing to deserve what I did to her, but at the time, I could not have cared less.

I moved into an efficiency apartment in a nearby high-rise building, only accessible by a special resident's card. With the fear for my safety dramatically heightened, I wanted to live in the most secure place I could afford.

Depressed and painfully lonely, longing for a sense of familiarity and comfort, I unwisely resumed my relationship with Greg.

Greg knew all my vulnerabilities. He knew about all my disappointments. He had watched me struggle to make financial ends meet for two years. We were in a relationship when I totaled my car so he knew about the two-thousand-dollar insurance settlement I had received.

The wheels in his crafty mind began to turn. Greg, who could not seem to make any of his own money, devised a plan to help me make more. It made no sense.

Before we broke up, he had become friends with a pawn shop owner who supposedly bought and sold gold, among other things.

Greg advised me that it took money to make money, and claimed that if he could use my two thousand dollars to buy and sell some gold, he could double it in just a few hours.

His plan, just as everything else he did, sounded convoluted and shady; certainly not something I wanted to risk all my money on.

But Greg would not let the subject die. He pleaded with me to allow him to help me. He tried to lay guilt on me about how hurt and insulted my lack of trust in him made him feel. He reminded me that in the two years I had known him, he had never stolen anything from me.

He intensely pressured me for three days until he finally got me to cave. I told him I would only risk half my savings—one thousand dollars. He swore on his life he would not rip me off. He even suggested I go with him to the place where he would do the exchange so I did not have to sit home and worry.

The next day, I cashed one thousand dollars out of the bank and drove Greg to the fast food restaurant where he had arranged to make the deal. I reluctantly handed him the cash and nervously waited in the car while he went inside.

A few minutes later, he came walking out of the restaurant, got into the passenger seat of my car, and handed me two thousand dollars cash. I don't know exactly how he pulled it off, but the fact that he did astonished me.

After proving he could deliver on his promise, he immediately put the pressure back on me again. He claimed if I gave him the entire three thousand dollars, he could just as easily turn it into six thousand dollars.

Perfectly content with the extra thousand dollars he had already made for me, I told him no.

He pressured me for a few more days until he finally convinced me to give him the entire three thousand dollars.

I told him how nervous I felt gambling with the only money I had. He said he understood, but swore on his life, again, that he would never rip me off. He promised I had nothing to worry about—I could trust him.

The next day, in complete opposition to my better judgment, I cashed out the other thousand dollars and apprehensively handed three thousand dollars over to him. He promised to return with six thousand dollars in just a few hours.

I stayed at home, waiting on pins and needles, for his return.

Several hours passed with no word from him. I began to worry a little but tried to convince myself that any number of things could have caused the delay.

I waited for the rest of the day, even stayed up late anticipating his return, but he never came back. I went to bed panicking and praying he would show up the next day.

The next day came and went. Days turned into weeks and weeks to months. I never heard from or saw Greg again. He vanished, seemingly off the face of the earth, and took my money with him. I could not understand how someone who professed to love me could betray me in such a cruel way.

I hit rock bottom. I felt worthless, hopeless, and shattered. I had no faith that things in my life would ever turn around.

I had yet to recognize the part I had played in the tragic trajectory of my life. And I felt powerless to redirect the course of it. It seemed nothing would change unless someone came along and changed it for me.

I clung desperately to the only hope I could think of—the only hope I believed I had left. One day, my knight in shining armor would arrive on his white horse, sweep me off my feet, and carry me off into the sunset.

Then everything ever wrong in my life would be right again.

> A few years later, when I learned about the signs and symptoms of drug addiction, all Greg's behavior began to make sense. I had stumbled upon drug paraphernalia twice; I found a syringe under the seat of my car, and a burnt spoon in one of my shoeboxes. He explained them both away and I believed him.

Showing Up to My Party

....

*The meeting of two personalities is like the
contact of two chemical substances; if there is any
reaction, both are transformed.* ~Carl Jung

....

Pop-culture took a dramatic turn in the 1980s with the emergence of disco music. Disco clubs sprang up everywhere. Girls with big hair-dos dolled up in dresses, and guys in fitted three-piece suits with barely buttoned shirts flocked to the clubs to socialize, drink, and dance.

My girlfriends and I often went to discos on the weekends hoping to meet nice guys to dance with and date. The dating part rarely panned out. Most of the guys at the clubs were alcoholics, cocaine addicts, or narcissistic losers.

Christopher's, a new club in my area, had recently opened. They booked the best local bands and gained instant popularity with the twenty-something single crowd.

One Saturday night while my girlfriend Darla and I were hanging out at Christopher's, a group of guys we had known from high school came walking in. I had gone there enough times to know the regulars but had never seen those particular guys there before. I could tell by their casual clothing that they had not come to dance; probably just to play the Pac-Man machine in an adjacent room.

We greeted them and I stood and chatted with them for a minute or two. Then I walked away to use the ladies room. Darla stayed there talking with them.

My interaction with the guys had been so brief, I did not notice the one guy in the group I had never met before. But he noticed me.

After I walked away, he asked Darla if I had a boyfriend. She told him I did not. He handed her a napkin and asked her to please write down my telephone number so he could call me.

When I met back up with Darla, the guys had already left the club. It took me by surprise to hear that one of them had asked about me and wanted my telephone number. In the midst of so many over-inflated egos, I found his modest approach adorable and refreshing.

Darla told me the guy's name was Keith and insisted I knew of him, but I had no recollection of knowing anything about him.

She reminded me about the part she played in the show our junior class put on for the graduating seniors six years ago, when we each parodied the personality of an upper classmen.

She re-enacted her role for me. "Keith is *so* cute. Keith is *so* wonderful. Keith is *so* rich."

"That's him. That's Lauren's ex-boyfriend, Keith!"

I knew Lauren but I did not remember knowing anything about her boyfriend.

Darla forewarned me that she may have given Keith an incorrect telephone number because I had recently changed it and she didn't know it very well. I really hoped she had not. I wanted to know more about him.

A week went by without Keith calling. I didn't know if he had changed his mind or just had the wrong phone number, but it disappointed me. I could not get the thought of him out of my head but did not know why.

A few weeks later, my class of 1976 had a five-year high school reunion. Darla and I went together.

As the reunion came to a close, I asked someone who I knew stayed connected with lots of people in the area if any parties were happening that night. He told me his older brother had gone to a party at his friend Keith's house and that I might want to check it out.

I could not believe what I had just heard. I knew it had to be the same Keith that Darla had given my number to, because the older brother he referred to was one of the guys in the group at Christopher's.

I told Darla about Keith's party and she agreed we should check it out. I could not wait to meet the mystery man face to face and find out why he never called me.

When we arrived at Keith's house, partygoers were overflowing from his backyard onto the street alongside it. With the door to the wooden privacy fence open, I could see a large crowd of people standing around a built-in swimming pool.

The second I stepped through the gate, a guy grabbed me by the arm. "Come with me, I've got to find Keith!"

He led me up the back steps of the house, through the kitchen, and into the living room.

Minutes later, a really cute guy with the sweetest brown eyes I had ever seen came walking toward me. His face beamed as he smiled from ear to ear.

He hugged me tight. "I can't believe you showed up to *your* party!" I looked at him, perplexed.

He explained. "After your friend gave me your number, I planned this party thinking you would be my date. But the phone number your friend gave me must have been wrong. Since that night, I have asked everyone I could think of who might know you if they knew how I could get in touch with you, but no one did."

Keith ran and grabbed a pen. "Tell me your number. I promise I will write it permanently on my hand so I will never ever lose it." He wrote my telephone number in blue ink on the palm of his hand.

I told him I could not stay because I had a friend with me.

He promised he would call me tomorrow. We hugged each other goodbye and he kissed me gently on my cheek. I found Darla in the crowd and we left.

The next evening, around eight o'clock, my telephone rang. I answered the call and said "Hello." A tender voice on the other end softly responded, "Hi, Baby."

I thought I would melt into a puddle on the floor.

Keith apologized for not calling earlier but explained that his friend had been rushed to the hospital and he had just gotten home. He asked when he could see me, if tomorrow evening would be okay. I told him that sounded great.

He arranged to pick me up around six o'clock in the evening, bring me back to his house, and cook dinner for us.

"There are some things you need to know about me, and I want to be the first to tell you. I'll pick you up tomorrow at six. I can't wait to see you. Sleep well, baby."

I hung up the phone and stretched out on the sofa, intoxicated by that dreamy conversation. I just wanted to lie there forever and bask in the feeling. I could not help but wonder if I had actually met the knight in shining armor I had been hoping for.

Keith arrived at my apartment building at six o'clock sharp the next evening. He had parked his pale-yellow Lincoln Continental right outside the front door of the building. I have to admit how much it impressed me that he drove such a nice car.

Keith lived in a quiet, older community called Silver Creek, on the corner of Cliffedge Road and Judy Lane, just a few miles from my apartment building.

As I followed him up the concrete steps leading up to his house, I could not help but notice how neglected the front lawn appeared. The overgrown evergreen trees had roots so large they had replaced most of the grass. He had no landscaping to speak of. The dirt beds against the house were dry and cracked.

As Keith showed me the inside of the house, I took a mental inventory.

Stepping through the front door, I immediately recognized how desperately the house needed a woman's touch.

Dated gold-marbled mirror squares covered one wall of the small living room. The only two pieces of furniture in there were an ugly brown velour sofa and a wood and glass coffee table. A half-dead plant sat inside the bay window.

He explained that his parents, who he claimed "used to be poor", had raised him and his brother there.

When his parents decided to move to a nicer home, Keith and his ex-wife Lauren, the girl I knew from school, bought the house.

I followed him up a steep staircase facing the front door in the living room. The house, a Cape Cod-style, had two windowed dormer rooms upstairs, one on each side.

The pitched ceilings in both rooms were covered with glossy black paint; the walls and floors in shag carpeting. It looked atrocious.

Back downstairs, a short hallway led from the living room to another bedroom. Keith pointed out that he had knocked out the wall between the original two smaller rooms to make one larger one.

The room seemed awkwardly long. A king-sized bed overfilled the right side. The left side of the room had a hodgepodge of unrelated furnishings.

The only closet in the room had no clothing hanging in it. Keith had removed the doors and used the space for his stereo equipment.

Continuing the tour, I followed him down an unfinished wooden stairway leading to the basement.

The walls of the basement front room were paneled in knotty pine. The room featured a large built-in bar paneled in the same. Rusty-orange colored shag carpeting covered the floor.

The unfinished left side of the basement had the typical gray concrete block walls and stained concrete slab floor. A clothes washer, dryer, and utility sink in the back-left corner delineated the laundry room.

Piled haphazardly on folding tables in the back of the room were a life-sized Santa-Claus doll, an old vibrating chin/neck firmer, and an open cardboard box filled to the top with baseball cards. I am sure there were many other things on the tables I did not notice at first glance.

Out-dated clothing left by his parents hung on metal rods suspended by chains from wooden studs. One dangling light bulb socket with a pull chain and two small casement windows covered in cobwebs provided minimal lighting for the entire room.

We left the basement and I followed him back upstairs to the kitchen.

The tiny kitchen had never been modernized. It still had its original white metal cabinets and a weirdly patterned white countertop.

A small dining area cluttered with an over-sized table and six large chairs stood adjacent to the kitchen.

The kitchen door led outside to the backyard/pool area; the one I had noticed the night of the party.

No doubt Keith had concentrated all his efforts on beautifying the country club-style backyard, by far the best feature of the house.

The yard had been cemented over and covered in bright green Astroturf. A spacious in-ground swimming pool spanned almost the entire width of the property. A well-tended landscaping bed inside the privacy wooden fence adorned the perimeter of the yard.

Begonias spilled over the sides of two planters, and a basket of impatiens hung from the arm of a white, ornamental light post.

A graying old cat lazily wandered around back there. Keith picked the cat up and introduced him to me. "I'd like you to meet Leon."

I reached over and pet the cat's head. "Well, hello, Leon. It's nice to meet you."

"Do you want to know why I named him Leon?" Keith asked me, grinning.

"I was wondering. That's a really funny name for a cat," I answered, grinning back at him.

"He used to be my friend's cat, but she moved and could not take him with her so I adopted him."

"Come on, Leon, smile." He gently opened the cat's mouth. "I named him after the boxer, Leon Spinks, because they are both missing their front teeth. See?"

I started giggling. "That's hilarious! What a perfect name!"

He put Leon back down on the ground and he scampered off.

An early July evening, the sun still shone brightly in the sky. He had already set a table for two, poolside and prepared a delicious meal. The atmosphere could not have been more perfect for a first date.

Keith had so many things he wanted to share with me. He said that the first time he saw me at Christopher's he declared to his friends, "See that girl, I'm going to marry her."

He went on to say that he somehow knew we were meant to be together. Then when I magically appeared at his house the night of his party, he received confirmation.

He asked if I liked baseball. I explained that I had gone to a baseball game or two with friends but had never really gotten into the sport.

He gushed, "I love baseball. I'm going to take you to all the Oriole games with me. You will love it too."

Then he gently touched my blonde hair, and mused, "I have a dream. One day I'm going to have a little blonde-haired daughter who I will name Cammy. I'll take her to all the Oriole games with me and hold her little hand while we walk down the stadium steps to our seats. We'll wear matching baseball caps. She will look so cute in her little hat."

I had never heard a guy share those kinds of dreams before. It deeply touched my heart to know how much the idea of fatherhood meant to him.

He continued. "I cannot stop thinking about you. I know we are supposed to be together and I want you in my life more than you can imagine. I brought you here so I could explain a part of my past you probably are not aware of. Before we go any further, I owe it to you to be honest."

Everything seemed so perfect up to that moment. Short of murder, I could not conceive of any admission of guilt that could possibly change that. I hoped the circumstances behind his confession would not be nearly as severe as he intimated.

Keith began. "I admitted myself into the Sheppard Pratt Hospital drug rehab program one year ago. I had lost control of my life and desperately needed help with my heroin addiction. I spent one month as an inpatient in that program. Now I am in recovery."

He showed me the track mark scars up and down his arms. Though I saw the evidence, I could not wrap my mind around him being a drug addict.

Keith did not fit the profile of a heroin addict—at least not the way I envisioned it. But as far as I knew, I had never met one before. I conceptualized heroin addicts to be destitute bums stumbling around or passed out cold on the sidewalk somewhere.

By all appearances, Keith had everything going for him. He seemed to be successful, intelligent and hard-working. He was a nice-looking guy and had a great personality. I tried to picture him as a junkie but could not.

I asked him if he would ever use drugs again. He responded the way I have since learned all recovering addicts in twelve-step programs respond: "I'm not using today. I take it one day at a time." He could not, in all honesty, promise me more than that.

His answer crushed me, though I did not let on. I wanted him to tell me he had been cured, to assure me that he had left his drug problem forever in the past. I wanted him to affirm he would never use again. But he could not and would not say those words.

I had just met this incredible guy. I had no experience, no realistic point of reference in regard to heroin addiction. I only knew that I did not want to let Keith go. It seemed I had so much more to gain than to lose.

I had no doubt that destiny brought me and Keith, my knight in shining armor, together. This story had to have a happy ending. It just had to.

SKELETONS IN THE CLOSET

....

Everybody's got skeletons in their closet. Every once in a while, you've got to open up the closet and let the skeletons breathe. ~Tyler Perry

....

When I first met Keith, his older brother, Mike, had been locked up in the state penitentiary for drug-related crimes. Mike had a history of previous incarcerations, though I do not know how many. What little Keith told me about his brother scared me.

From what I could gather, the creep had a terrible reputation. I did not want to meet him.

Keith explained that he and his brother had always been polar opposites. He had been a sweet, sensitive child with a personality that drew people to him. Mike had none of those qualities and resented him for it.

Their social parents often left Mike, five years older, at home to babysit for Keith. Jealous over others' adoration of his younger brother, Mike systematically employed strategies to tarnish Keith's image. A masterful manipulator, he knew exactly how to hoodwink his parents. I don't know if they were blind to the problem or chose to ignore it.

One night after their parents had gone out, Keith's brother invited a few of his equally menacing friends over. With Mike acting as the ring leader, the older boys planned a surprise attack on Keith they all thought would be funny.

The boys pounced on Keith, only fourteen years old, pinned down his arms, and watched him helplessly struggle while Mike injected heroin into the vein in his arm.

Keith's entire life changed that night. Before long, Mike succeeded in getting him addicted to it.

Unaware of the underlying problem, Keith's parents could not control his burgeoning unruly behavior. Keith dropped out of high school at age sixteen and went to work at his father's produce market. Things continued to get worse.

Keith first loved the needle. As his addiction progressed, he added pills like Quaaludes, Dilaudid, Valium, and any other "downs" he could get a hold of. As his tolerance to the drugs increased, he would take handfuls at a time.

While driving under the influence, he wrecked car after car. Every time he wrecked one, his father would buy him a new one.

He met his ex-wife Lauren sometime between 1974 and 1975. She thought Keith was "rich" and that she had won the lottery.

In reality, Keith had no money of his own. It all belonged to his parents. But Lauren hooked her talons into him with no intention of letting go.

They had a troubled, drug-induced relationship based on co-addiction and drama, not love.

One weekend, the two of them went on a gambling trip to Las Vegas. They brought along a cache of drugs.

The first night of the trip, Lauren doled out the Quaaludes, deliberately giving Keith more than she planned to take herself. Then she dragged Keith, "trashed" and incoherent, off to a quickie-mart wedding chapel. Keith woke up the next morning with a wedding ring on his finger and without any recollection of how it had gotten there.

Keith and Lauren had lived together for two years but he had no intention of marrying her and she knew it. After the Las Vegas trip, he figured that as long as they were already married, he would try to make it work.

On June 9, 1978, they went to settlement on the Cliffedge Road house as co-owners. Her plan had succeeded; Lauren had legally tied herself to Keith in every way. But they had a predictably disastrous marriage.

Things got ugly fast. They provoked each other constantly and fought over everything. Sometimes their arguments turned into physical fights. In less than one year, their tempestuous marriage ended.

Since Lauren owned half of the Cliffedge Road house, Keith had no choice but to buy her out in the divorce settlement. On September 20, 1979, he became the sole owner of the property, forever free of her.

Keith learned a hard lesson and never forgot it.

All the Way

....

*Love recognizes no barriers. It jumps hurdles,
leaps fences, penetrates walls to arrive at its
destination full of hope.* ~Maya Angelou

....

Nothing seems insurmountable when two people are intoxicated with the feeling of falling in love. Without the conscious recollection of losing each other, it seemed Keith and I had found each other again. We were inseparable.

After just one date, our relationship hit the ground running. A few weeks later, my dog, Shane, and I moved into the Cliffedge Road house with Keith and his cat, Leon.

Keith had lots of friends and many interests. I had an entertaining and refreshing life with him.

He enjoyed playing his favorite record albums for me. Among his large, diversified collection, he had every Rolling Stones album ever released. He knew the words to all the songs which he sang with the confidence of a virtuoso but definitely not the talent of one. Keith did a comical impression of Mick Jagger's boastful strut. I could not watch his ridiculous antics without bursting into laughter.

He did a hilarious though not very good impression of Elvis

too. He loved listening to Elvis Presley's music and reading books about his life.

Keith also liked Barbra Streisand. He knew the words to every one of her songs and sang along with her. He had a terrible singing voice but did not care.

He also had a fascination with the music of Jim Morrison and the Doors. I believe he related his own addiction struggles to those Morrison expressed through his dark, poetic lyrics.

Keith had a special fondness for the Patti Austin/James Ingram album, "Every Home Should Have One". He told me that his favorite song on the album, "Baby Come to Me", which he played over and over, made him think of me. Whenever I hear that song on the radio today, it transports me back to that magical time and place in my life.

Wanting to know everything about me, Keith often asked me questions, sometimes making a game of it.

I remember both of us sitting cross-legged, facing each other on his ugly brown velour sofa. He began, "I'm going to ask you a question. Say the first thing that pops into your head. Don't think about it."

"What is your absolute favorite song ever written?"

"All The Way, sung by Frank Sinatra." The words sounded foreign as they emerged from my lips. I had no memory of ever considering or expressing that favoritism. But the emotive song had stayed with me ever since I had seen the movie "The Joker's Wild" as a child.

His eyes opened wide with surprise. "I cannot believe you just said that! I *love* that song." We both started singing the song—"*When somebody loves you, it's no good unless he loves you, All The Way.*"

For me, that brief discourse remains suspended in time. Neither of us knew just how defining that song would be in terms of our relationship.

Keith made me feel pampered and adored in a way no one ever had at a time in my life when I so desperately needed to feel that way.

Soon after we began dating, Keith asked me what my favorite fruit was. I told him I loved cherries but only firm and dark ones.

The next day, he surprised me at my job holding a brown paper bag with two pounds of large, perfect cherries; every single one firm, dark and washed. I could not imagine how long it took the girl at the market to sort through all the boxes to find the most perfect ones. I had never received such a thoughtful gift.

The romantic comedy "Arthur" starring Dudley Moore and Liza Minnelli opened in August 1981. Keith and I went to see it the first night it was out.

We both enjoyed the film but it especially struck an emotional chord in him. Later that evening, he professed that while watching the movie, he had fallen deeply in love with me.

Keith had such a sweet way about him. I felt like a princess in a fairytale. He indulged me, took care of my every need. I could relax, be myself, and know that he loved me unconditionally.

I breathed a huge sigh of relief. My painful, tumultuous past was finally behind me. I had found the serenity and happiness I had dreamed of for so long.

The Polaroid Picture

....

Important encounters are planned by the souls long before the bodies see each other. ~Paulo Coelho

....

Keith's father's produce market was not your ordinary, run of the mill fruit and vegetable stand. Years before I met Keith, his father had purchased a little road-side stand and the prime property it sat on.

Shortly after buying the business, the United Food and Commercial Workers Union Local 27 called a strike, forcing all the area unionized grocery stores to shut down until an agreement could be reached.

His privately owned, non-unionized market was the only place for local residents to shop. Within his first few months of ownership, he recouped his entire investment. The little produce market became a booming, multi-million-dollar business. He dreamed of one day turning it over to his sons.

As a produce buyer, Keith worked very odd hours. The Jessup wholesale market opened at ten p.m. Sunday through Friday. The freshest produce and best deals were had in the early hours of the morning.

Sunday through Thursday, Keith went to bed at seven p.m.

sharp and woke up at two a.m. in the morning. Then he and his father would do all the buying for the day, go back to the business, and then come home at around eleven o'clock in the morning.

I worked retail hours; nine to five or twelve to nine, five days a week.

After a month of living together, we got tired of our conflicting work schedules. Since we really didn't need my income, we both agreed I should quit my job.

With my newly found free time, I took on the project of getting the badly neglected house in shape. The only closet on the first floor was already bursting at the seams. I had no place to hang my clothes.

A large walk-in closet upstairs between the dormers had not been used, probably since Lauren had moved out. Trash covered every square inch of the floor. I decided to clean it up and claim it for my own.

I marched in there armed with several big black trash bags and a vacuum cleaner. Then I plopped myself down on the floor and went to work.

Random papers littered the closet floor, so I began the task of separating the keepers from the trash. While going through one particular pile, I came across the back of a buried Polaroid picture. I pulled it out of the pile and flipped it over.

I could not believe my eyes; it was a picture of me! The scenario came back to me when I saw the background of the picture and the clothing I had on. I remembered Lauren taking that snapshot six years before at my high-school boyfriend's senior prom. They had both been in the same graduating class.

Assuming she had left more than one picture, I searched through all the papers on the floor. I rummaged through everything but never found another snapshot.

That picture of me had been hidden in Keith's house for years without him even knowing it existed. He had never seen my face or at least remembered seeing it before the night he had first noticed me at Christopher's. What were the odds?

After clearing out the closet, I set my sights on the rest of the house. Keith barely knew how to change a light bulb nor did he have the motivation to do so. Any changes would be up to me.

A lady who had worked for his family for many years came once a week to clean the house and do the laundry. I appreciated having someone do the housework but I could not stand having her around because of her acute body odor problem.

I would walk in the house hours after she left and the foul odor would smack me right in the face. It did not seem to bother Keith at all. He wanted a clean house and laundered clothes and did not care who did it.

I weighed the options of tolerating the odor or doing the housework, a chore I despised, by myself. I decided she had to go.

Since I had no job, I contributed by cooking dinner each night. I had been a pescatarian for several years. Keith enjoyed many of the foods I ate, but he occasionally wanted meat or chicken for dinner.

Whenever I prepared those meals for him, I wore rubber dishwashing gloves because I could not stand to touch the raw flesh.

I would have done anything to make Keith happy; to show my appreciation. He treated me so well.

Comic Relief

....

Every girl deserves a guy that can make her heart forget it was ever broken. ~Kurt Smith

....

I had never experienced dining out quite the way I did with Keith. The first restaurant he ever took me to, The Palmer House, had been named for the daily palm/tarot card readings made available to its patrons. A spiritualist sat at a table in the front and gave readings upon request for fifteen dollars.

In its heyday, The Palmer House, a nostalgic, family-owned Italian restaurant, had attracted special occasion diners for elegant candlelit meals. Faded autographed photos of by-gone celebrity patrons lined the walls. The restaurant's swanky appeal had long since gone by the wayside, leaving a much humbler clientele. Neighborhood regulars frequented the eatery where "everybody knew your name".

The owners had been produce customers of Keith's father for many years. His parents ate there practically every week. With the friendship came a dining experience that far surpassed that of the average patron.

On the evening of my first visit to The Palmer House, we were greeted at the door with a warm welcome and then seated at a table in the back. I never saw a menu. Keith ordered all of his favorites for me to try.

The Palmer House had delicious food with plentiful portions; way more than we could eat in one sitting. Keith knew that but he liked to order a variety of dishes and then take doggy bags home for another day.

Keith loved nice clothes. I had never met a guy who liked shoes more or had a larger inventory than I did. Whenever we went out, he wore a sports jacket and matching shoes.

He once showed me a box filled with a collection of platform shoes he had saved from the seventies. Though they looked like shoes Elton John would have worn as part of a flashy costume on stage, Keith actually wore them as daily foot attire. The colors ranged from pink plaid to yellow patent leather, and all the platforms were three inches or higher. I could only imagine what he looked like stepping out in those monstrosities. The thought of it cracked me up.

I had a stimulating and fun life with Keith. He added color and comic relief to my previously troubled life.

Keith had lots of friends and his house had always been their hangout. I liked the majority of them and did not mind that we always had visitors.

He had two very close friends who were brothers to each other and like brothers to him. I had already known those guys pretty well before I'd met Keith. They lived in my old neighborhood and we had all gone to school together. I felt comfortable having them around the house.

Keith and I enjoyed playing backgammon. We would play the game whenever no guests were over.

He also liked playing word-memory games. One game in particular began by naming one type of animal and then taking turns adding onto the chain of words. For instance, one hen, two cows, three tigers, four giraffes, five ducks, and so on. He had an awesome memory and could go on and on. I, on the other hand, could never get past the fifth animal. He assured me I would get better with practice but I never did.

Keith was a math whiz and loved calculating baseball statistics. He would sit on the sofa with a yellow lined legal pad, diligently making columns and lists of complicated statistical problems to figure out. Watching his keen mind in action, I often imagined how different his life might have been had he stayed in school and applied himself.

I simply could not understand why someone with so much potential had been hell-bent on self-destruction. Since I had only seen him at his best, I could not visualize him at his worst. I never wanted to experience the silent demon that he battled every day, and prayed that his addiction would never resurface.

I believed that I had the power to keep him sober; that if I loved him enough, he would never want to use again.

My life with Keith could not have been better. Only one thing concerned me. All the addiction and recovery literature I had read stated that alcohol compromised sobriety. Keith, a far cry from an alcoholic, had occasional drinks at restaurants, maybe more when we went out with his parents. He never drank at home.

He assured me that he did not have a problem with alcohol and that I had nothing to worry about.

From what I had observed, that seemed to be true. Still, it concerned me. But since he functioned so well in every aspect of his life, I did not want to place too much emphasis on the social drinking. I had no experience when it came to addiction and did not want to be the judge of his behavior. If he ensured me that things were okay, I had to believe him.

Keith and I often dined out with his parents. I got along well with them and enjoyed their company. They were a comical, entertaining couple. I never knew what to expect from our evenings together but I always looked forward to the show.

Habitually between five and six o'clock every evening, his parents would have one round of Scotch on the rocks at home. Then they would go out to a restaurant, sit at the bar, and continue drinking Scotch until they were ready to eat dinner. The more they drank, the drunker and funnier they got.

After we sat down at a table, his parents would inevitably find a trivial point of contention to argue. Both of them loud and flagrant, they would banter back and forth across the dinner table, neither one admitting they were wrong. Eventually, realizing that no one could win, his mother would begin her storytelling. She would recall situations from her ordinary daily affairs and exaggerate them.

She thrived on attention; the more reaction she received, the more outrageous the stories became. She would repeat the same story over and over, more histrionic with each reprise.

Keith's parents lived in a beautiful high-rise condo in Baltimore and had a second home in Boca Raton, Florida. His mother enjoyed Florida much more than she did Baltimore, and therefore, spent six months of the year there. His father stayed behind with his produce business. He thrived on working hard and did not like being away from his business for extended periods of time.

Keith had obviously gotten his fashion sense from his father. His dad always dressed beautifully. He wore a brand-new shirt every time he went out—he would only wear a shirt once and then give it away. He had an extensive hat and shoe collection that matched every outfit he wore.

His father had a loud, intimidating roar but a loving, generous nature. He owned several cars, mostly Lincolns and Cadillacs that he distributed among friends and family. He demanded impeccable service wherever he went, but those who cared for him were heavily rewarded.

Keith's parents belonged to the very exclusive Boca Raton Hotel and Beach Club in Florida. They owned a magnificent Rolls Royce Corniche convertible that his mother drove all around Boca.

His mother, a stunning, petite blonde with a perpetual dark suntan, spent her days at the club relaxing in her private cabana or floating on her raft in the ocean or pool. She sparkled from head to toe with diamond jewelry which included the beautiful necklace that spelled out her name "Boots" in diamonds. Every stylish outfit she wore had studded rhinestones on it.

I am not sure who had more hats and shoes; her or her husband. She shuffled around in her backless high heel shoes, taking small steps to keep her balance. Her perfectly manicured fingernails were never less than an inch long. Everywhere she went, people knew her by name.

Keith's mother had an outrageous personality. She never filtered her words. No subject was taboo. A very kind-hearted, charitable woman, she volunteered her time and contributed a significant amount of money to animal causes.

Keith referred to his parents by their first names (actually nicknames); Boots and Kope. He never called them Mom and Dad. They did not seem to mind, though I thought it sounded cold and disrespectful.

I think his parents had become anesthetized after going through so many painful ordeals with him. Drug addiction by nature destroys the trust and respect of all relationships.

But the more time we all spent together, the more loving their interactions became. I saw their relationships turn around in just a few short months.

With me in the picture, his parents gradually let down their guard and regained a guarded level of trust with him. It touched my heart deeply the first time I heard Keith call his parents Mom and Dad. I felt it showed tremendous growth on his part.

While both his parents were in Baltimore, Keith swept me away for a trip to sunny Florida. I had vacationed in Miami as a young child and spent a few days in Ft. Lauderdale, but I had never experienced the "Boca" life.

For one utopian week, I had the opportunity to walk in his mother's shoes, madly in love and surrounded by swaying palm trees. We had first-class accommodations at his parents' golf villa apartment on the grounds of the grandiose old Boca Raton Hotel.

As an extension of the main hotel, their apartment included maid service and clean linens daily.

His mother had taken her Rolls Royce to Baltimore so we drove the Lincoln Continental that remained in Florida.

Keith and I went to the Beach Club every day that week. Only members or hotel guests were permitted to enter the property through the security gate. Each day, we drove our car up to the gate just like VIPs, mentioned his mother's name to the security guard, and sailed right through. Then we would do the same with the valet at the club and he would park our car right up front.

Keith's parents had given us carte blanche with their hotel account. We just showed the card and everything went on their bill.

The first day we were there, Keith turned me on to the most luscious piña colada I had ever tasted. We subsequently indulged in the twelve-dollar frozen cocktails every day for the rest of the week.

For lunch, the dining room offered a massive, pricey salad bar as well as a variety of overpriced tropical menu items. Outside, on the dining room patio, a Latin guitarist serenaded the guests with calypso music.

Every evening we would dress up and go to one of his favorite restaurants for dinner. I had the time of my life on that vacation. I tasted a lifestyle I never thought I would be privy to and I loved every second of it. Who wouldn't?

I liked Keith's parents and they liked me. I had yet to meet his incarcerated brother. Keith rarely mentioned him. No one ever had a kind word to say about the guy so I felt no great loss.

One autumn weekday afternoon, Keith and I took a drive to Western Maryland to see the spectacularly colored trees on the mountainside. While we were up there, I suggested we stop in Hagerstown so I could show him a beautiful park I had once visited.

Greenbrier State Park, nestled in the Appalachian Mountains, had a fifty-acre lake. In the summer, it offered swimming and sunbathing on its sandy beach. Now fall, the weather had turned cool and the swimming season had ended. The air felt crisp and cool but the sun reflecting off the lake felt warm.

Off-season and midweek, the expansive beach was deserted. We shared the quiet setting with one other person, a photographer trying to capture the breathtaking scenery on film.

Feeling romantic, we took off our shoes and walked hand-in-hand along the beach. The guy with the camera asked if he could take our picture. We did not know why he wanted it but considered his request a compliment.

A few days later, Keith received a collect call from his brother, Mike, at the Maryland Correctional Institution who had called to say that when he received his weekly copy of the Hagerstown Herald-Mail, it had our picture on the front cover. He congratulated Keith on his new girlfriend.

I never asked Keith when his brother would be released. I did not look forward to that dreadful homecoming.

First and Foremost an Addict

....

When I eventually met Mr. Right, I had no idea that his first name was "always". ~Rita Rudner

....

Our family of four had settled into a happy, comfortable lifestyle together. Shane and Leon were happy having free run of the house and backyard. Keith and I both loved animals so we decided to get another dog.

He thought Basset Hounds were cute because of their sad droopy eyes, but I wanted something a bit cuddlier.

He agreed to go check out a litter of puppies I had seen advertised in the paper. Once we saw the puppies, we had to have one. The adorable little fur-balls were a mix of Black Labrador Retrievers and Irish Setters. We already had two boys so we picked out a cute, friendly female pup and brought her home.

Her sweet little face inspired the name Honeybell. We named her after our favorite orange.

Shane seemed a bit unnerved when he first met Honeybell but she soon became his best friend. Lazy Leon could not have cared less as long as she did not try to sniff him. He hid most of the time anyway.

Before we knew it, our little black puffball had turned into a man-size dog. On her two feet, she stood as tall as we did. She loved to jump up, put her big paws on our shoulders, and hang on while we danced with her.

Our little "family" had grown and we had established ourselves as a couple. We were both wholeheartedly invested in our future together.

Keith asked me to get a part-time job. It had nothing to do with money; he just wanted me to use my time more productively. I had no case to argue. He suggested working as a cashier at his father's produce market and I agreed to give it a shot.

Long story short, I hated that job. In an effort not to show favoritism among his employees, Keith patronized me. I did not appreciate his condescending tone, nor did I enjoy freezing my butt off while standing on the cold, concrete slab for hours at a time.

I liked cashiering, but in my idle time, I had to trim up vegetables and package spinach, among other things. The cold, wet, dirty spinach came in boxes. I had to reach my hands into that muck and make up one-pound bags for sale. My fingers froze and my fingertips shriveled up. Wet, sandy grime imbedded under my fingernails. I detested *everything* about that filthy task.

I did not work there very long.

Since my prior work experience had been in bookkeeping, I thought it best to direct my search to those kinds of jobs.

I found a part-time job working in the home office of a locally-based retail sports apparel chain. Two friendly young women worked in the office full-time. I already knew one of the women from high school.

The office had an upbeat environment and I did not have to travel far to get there.

With Keith at home all day, his friends often came over to hang out. I would come home around two o'clock on my working days and then we would spend the rest of the afternoon together.

One day after work, I walked through the front door and found the living room in shambles. I thought for sure our house had been robbed and ransacked. The room looked as if a cyclone had raged through it.

Our potted palm tree was lying on its side with its dirt spilled out onto the carpet. A hanging picture had crashed onto the floor, glass broken and fragments perilously scattered. The empty frame of the wooden coffee table leaned on its side against the mirrored wall; its quarter-inch-thick, cracked glass-top leaned next to it.

As I surveyed the damage, Keith came stumbling in from the bedroom, his glassy eyes trying to focus and his drooping eyelids fighting to stay open.

Doped up, struggling to get the words out, he droned, "I'm sorrrry. I messssed uuup."

In that instant, my fairytale turned into a nightmare. I felt totally betrayed.

Hysterically crying, I shouted "What have you done? Look at you, you're completely fucked up."

He moronically blabbered, "So—what—I—had—a—slip. It haaapens to everybody."

"Look what you did," I clamored through heavy sobs! "You are sickening!"

My impassioned words landed on deaf ears. Too incoherent to reason with, I somberly watched as he staggered over to the sofa, plopped down, then slumped over and passed out.

I ran to the bedroom, sprawled out on the bed, and dissolved into tears. I cried until my stomach hurt and my eyes had swollen nearly shut. Suffering alone, the pain seemed unbearable. The one person I had always counted on had become the source of my agony. And he lay bombed out and drooling on the living room sofa.

I recognized Keith's revolting "luded-out" behavior because I had seen other people on Quaaludes act that way. I did not know who his cohorts were that day, but it infuriated me to think that a "friend" would sell drugs to a recovering addict. Didn't they care about his sobriety?

Though seeing Keith in that state devastated me, I could not bring myself to give up on him for one exercise in poor judgment. I only hoped that the sober realization of what he had put me through would quell any future compulsions to use.

I decided that from that point on, I would shower him with enough love to insure his desire to stay straight for me. He had given so much of himself to me. Now it was my turn to stick by him and prove my devotion.

When he came out of his drug haze, I poured my heart out to him. I tried to make him understand how the sight of him in that state had crushed me. I wanted him to console me, promise me I would never have to suffer through that kind of hell again.

He held me and deeply apologized for hurting me that way. I felt so relieved to have him back to normal, to share my feelings with him.

My sweetheart would surely promise he would never do that to me again. He would tell me that he loved me too much to ever hurt me and that our relationship meant more to him than any drug possibly could. But even as he witnessed my suffering, he could not in good conscience promise me any of those things.

He was first and foremost a drug addict, and therefore, lived his life one day at a time.

Only Shooting Water

....

Insanity is when you love someone so much you help them destroy you by trying to save them. ~Jaskamal Singh

....

After the Quaalude incident, Keith and I resumed our life as if nothing had happened.

As far as I could tell, Keith had gotten back on track with his sobriety and I tried to forget that whole ugly mess. I just wanted to move forward in our relationship. We had so much going for us and an exciting future ahead.

We shared so many dreams. Things just had to work out. They just had to.

But I found it hard to view Keith the same way as I had before. I had seen Keith's other personality and I did not like it. I loved everything about "Normal Keith", but his flip side scared me. A stranger had stood before me that dreadful afternoon and I hated him. I did not welcome him back.

I don't know exactly how it happened but after that incident, our roles reversed. He stopped caring about my needs and I began taking full responsibility for his.

Keith knew he had a steadfast ally in me. And he knew that I would go to any lengths to keep our relationship together.

I remember him lecturing to me one day in an authoritative tone that "Having an adult relationship means keeping the details of our life private."

At the time, I thought that sounded so romantic. I did not realize he had begun laying the enabling groundwork.

From time to time, Keith went out early in the evening to play racquetball. When he came home, he always hung his canvas gym bag on the inside knob of the door leading down to the basement.

One morning, I had gathered up a load of towels to wash. Before heading down to the laundry room, I figured I would see if anything in his bag needed washing.

I unzipped it and looked inside. The bag was completely empty except for one thing: a hypodermic needle lying on the bottom.

There could only be one reason for Keith to carry a needle around or hide one in there. He was using again.

I furiously glared at the needle, sickened by the thought of Keith sticking it in his vein.

He had not come home from work yet so I couldn't confront him. That drove me crazy. I paced the floors in delirium, blinded by the rage surging inside of me. I felt as if I would burst if he didn't come home soon.

When Keith finally walked through the door, I ambushed him with the evidence. Manic after hours of waiting, I waved the needle in front of his face and screamed, "How could you do this to me?"

He did not appear flustered by the confrontation, just concerned with my anger.

"Shhhh. Calm down. It's not what you think. Everything is okay. Give me a chance to explain," he appealed with a soothing voice.

"Explain? What is there to explain?" I shouted back. There's only one reason why you would have a needle in your gym bag."

"Shhh, listen—everything's okay. I'm not using."

I stopped screaming and allowed him the chance to explain.

"I know you will find this hard to believe, but I only used water.

When I got off heroin, I never lost the urge to feel the needle. That's all I did, I promise. You have nothing to be worried about. It will all be okay. Please don't be upset."

Like a light switch, my focus changed from my pain to his. Though I found the thought of what he had just revealed to me very disturbing, he had obviously been struggling with his sobriety. He needed understanding, not condemnation. I beat myself up for being so hard on him.

Keith's lame explanation eased my mind because that is what I wanted to hear. I took him at his word without questioning the validity of his reasoning. Poking holes in his story could mean the demise of our relationship. I did not want that to happen.

As long as "Normal Keith" stood before me, I chose to look the other way.

After that day, Keith began drilling me daily with "what if" questions, trying to test my level of devotion. I hated the drills but tried to ease his mind by responding the way I knew he wanted me to.

The question "If I ever got locked up, would you be there for me—no matter what?" disturbed me the most. I could not imagine that happening and assured him I would be there for him—no matter what.

One morning, not more than a few weeks after the gym bag incident, I climbed the stepstool looking for something I had placed in the back of the highest kitchen cabinet. Standing on the third step, I could see straight into the bottom shelf of the cabinet.

Lying on the edge just inside the door was another hypodermic needle. I could tell that he had reached up there in a hurry, barely getting his fingers past the edge. He had clearly made an effort to hide the evidence.

The shock of seeing another syringe sent me spiraling into panic mode. Keith had not come home from work yet, so I had to wait to confront him again.

When he finally walked through the front door after I had

fervently obsessed for hours, my pent-up anxiety exploded like a time bomb. Brandishing the incriminating evidence, I ambushed him again.

He remained perfectly composed just as he had the time before. He even used the same lame "water" excuse. I questioned his alibi but no matter how hard I pushed, he would not admit to anything.

Though overcome with my own pain, fear, and disappointment, I once again brushed my feelings aside and focused on his needs.

I blamed myself; I should have been more loving. I should have tried harder to keep him happy. I should have been more diligent in keeping him sober.

I believed I was much stronger and better equipped to shoulder the burden of his addiction than he was.

Unable to recall any recent signs of drug abuse, I asked him about his sobriety once more for reassurance. He assured me I had nothing to worry about.

Having heard what I wanted to hear, I slipped right back into denial.

Willful Disregard

....

A relationship without trust is like a car without gas. You can stay in it all you want, but it won't go anywhere. ~Michael J. Herbert

....

The secure foundation I had come to rely on in my relationship with Keith had crumbled into dust. Knowing my entire world could crash down around me at any time, I lived every moment stressed out and worried.

My needs no longer mattered to me or him. My entire life centered on fixing his problems.

Keith had become noticeably irresponsible. He could not seem to stay out of trouble. I kept finding speeding tickets haphazardly lying around the house. He had also amassed a collection of parking tickets. He never worried about those kinds of things. His lawyer always managed to have them "taken care of".

His attorney, also a highly respected County Councilman, had become well-known among young, white-collar drug offenders who relied on him to have their charges dismissed.

His public service position afforded him lots of privileges and favors. Keith told me that his lawyer used those perks to defend his premium clients and sacrificed his low-income clients in exchange.

I found Keith's willful disregard for the law frustrating. I could not understand why he did not even flinch in the face of it.

Though I often pleaded with him to clean up his act, he refused to listen to me and smugly continued to buck the system.

Whenever I brought the subject up, he would confidently assert that he had everything under control. It never looked that way to me. Then again, I had no experience in that area. Thankfully, I had not personally dealt with the court system. But maybe street-wise Keith knew something I did not. I could only watch, worry, and hope.

My girlfriend, Jane, a friend since elementary school, owned a house in the neighborhood we lived in. I got together with her from time to time.

One particular evening, knowing Keith had plans with friends, Jane and I arranged for a "girls' night out". She offered to drive.

Keith did not know when he would be leaving. He was still home when Jane arrived to pick me up. I kissed him goodbye and told him to have a great time.

We hung out at Jane's house for a little while and then decided to head downtown.

Driving around the streets of downtown Baltimore, looking for a place to park, I noticed a green Pontiac Lemans, just like the one I drove, parked on the opposite side of the road. Police cruisers with flashing lights were parked in front of and behind it.

Keith had not asked or had any reason to use my car that night, but I had a dreadful feeling he had gotten himself into trouble.

I asked Jane to do a u-turn and drive me across the street.

She pulled her car behind the police cruiser and I jumped out. I checked the license plate to see if it was my car. Sure enough, it was.

I asked the officer what had happened. He told me that the gentleman driving the car had been arrested for a DUI. Another squad car had recently transported him to Central Booking.

I explained to him that I owned the car and asked if I could drive it home. He told me I could not. Since the car had been involved in a crime, it had to be impounded.

I reflected on the timing of events. Keith had to have left the house immediately after I did to have gotten downtown before us. That sneaky son of a bitch sat there cool, calm, and collected as I hugged him goodbye, knowing full well that the minute I left he was going to take my car downtown on a drug run.

I hated what he had done, but more than that, I hated that he had straight-faced lied to me. I felt betrayed, manipulated, and used.

Now I understood what the commitment drillings were about. He had been grooming me knowing full well he would do something to get himself locked up.

I wanted him to suffer for what he had done to me. I thought about leaving him in jail to sweat it out for a while but I feared his retaliatory anger. Somehow, he would turn the whole thing around and make it my fault.

No matter how angry he made me or how hurt I felt, I knew that Keith would expect me to hold up my side of the bargain. That meant I had to bail him out.

I got back in Jane's car and we headed to Central Booking at the downtown courthouse to try and get Keith released.

The courthouse building stood right in the heart of the most depraved part of town, infamously known as "The Block", well-known for its strip clubs, porno shops, and peep shows. Perverts, prostitutes, and vagabonds wandered the streets around there all hours of the night.

The area was not safe, especially for two twenty-something women. We found a parking space up the street and then quickly scurried toward the courthouse, passing a string of homeless people sleeping on the sidewalk.

Other indigents sat on the steps of the courthouse building panhandling for money. I never imagined I would end up in a place or situation like that. I resented Keith for putting me in that position.

Jane and I sat and waited several hours for Keith's case to be processed. Finally, the magistrate set his bail. I did not have enough money to pay it so Jane graciously offered to loan it to me. We paid his bail and then they released him.

I have no recollection of what I actually said to Keith that night, though I do remember his attitude. He never thanked me or seemed the least bit grateful for what I did for him. Bailing him out was part of our agreement and, therefore, expected of me.

In the days that followed the DUI incident, I tried everything I could think of to make Keith understand the proportion of my despair. I pleaded, cried, rationalized and threatened. I even tried to intellectualize addiction from his viewpoint. If I knew what the triggers were, maybe I could help him stay sober.

I knew that something deep, dark, and painful had to be gnawing at his insides, but he had no conscious awareness of what that something could be.

I finally reached the conclusion that he had no insight to share and no rationalization could be found. Addiction consumed him. He struggled with it every minute of every day.

Keith and I had shared so many beautiful dreams together and I did not want those dreams to die. I believed our relationship had been predestined and I would do whatever it took to make it work.

I saw the wonderful guy inside the addict drowning and I believed I had to save him.

Keith threw me a bone and promised to trust me more with his feelings. I accepted his promise and clung to the shred of hope that this nightmare would soon end.

Desperate Measures

....

You will never understand the damage you did to someone until the same thing is done to you. That's why I'm here. ~Karma

....

Keith kept me off balance and confused with his lies and manipulations. I did not know whether to trust my observations and instincts, or believe his fabrications and excuses. Each point of view demonstrated degrees of validity. One thing for sure, I no longer trusted him.

I kept our problems hidden from the outside world, enabled him and made excuses for his behavior. In a desperate attempt to keep our relationship intact, I averted conflict with him whenever possible.

I believed if I did and said everything perfectly, our relationship would eventually get back on track. That meant keeping him under my watchful eye every possible minute of every day. That oppressive burden fostered my withdrawal from friends and family.

Though unaware, I had become entangled in the web of codependency. It did not matter to me that I had lost myself in my relationship with Keith and his addiction. My entire life circled around his. I pacified him, monitored his sobriety, fixed his problems, and worked overtime trying to keep our relationship intact. I honestly believed I could manage all of it.

Keith seemed able to sustain weeks of sobriety before relapsing, though I could never really tell because he spent hours away from home each day and he never used in front of me. For all I knew, he used every day. I just did not want to believe that.

Dreading the next slip, I lived my life teetering on the emotional edge, believing I could somehow love him out of his addiction.

One evening, we went downtown to Little Italy to dine at Sabatino's, one of our favorite restaurants. We ordered our usual meals: two house salads and two baked rigatonis, well done.

Partway into the meal, I got up to use the ladies room, leaving Keith sitting at the table.

When I returned, I found Keith face down in his plate of baked rigatoni. I called his name and he looked up at me, his face covered with tomato sauce, in a drug-induced stupor. I know it sounds funny, the thought of it now makes me laugh, but at that moment, I did not see the humor in it. His sloppy, disgusting behavior humiliated me. I could not stand the sight of him.

I wanted to extricate myself from the situation as quickly as possible without making a scene.

I told Keith I was leaving and he could figure out how to get home on his own.

He threatened that if I left him there I had better find another place to live.

I motioned for the waiter to bring the check. Then I paid the bill and stormed away from the table. Keith followed me, stumbling and weaving the entire way.

The valet brought our car to the front of the restaurant and opened the passenger door. Keith fell into the front seat. Then alongside my bombed-out boyfriend, but all alone with my aching heart, I drove silently home.

The next day, Keith apologized for his behavior, professed his undying love for me, and promised to try harder; same old bullshit.

That's all it ever took to keep me coming back for more. I bought his crap every time,

Between incidents, he hid his addiction very well from me. Wanting to believe the nightmare had ended, I lived in a quixotic state of denial.

But when the financial resources supporting his habit dried up, he could no longer hide it from me. And I could look away no longer.

Each week, I deposited the money Keith gave me into my personal checking account and then used it to pay bills. Keith had no access to that account.

When my bank started offering a bounce-free checking service, I signed up for the option. In the event my account became overdrawn, a ten-thousand-dollar loan with interest would automatically be generated to cover the checks. I had no intention of letting that happen. I only took it as a precautionary measure.

One month, I opened my bank statement shocked to see that the ten-thousand-dollar over-draft loan had kicked in. Since I knew I had not overdrawn my account, I could only assume the bank had made an error.

I flipped through all the returned checks they had mailed back to me with my statement and found the evidence. Keith had written an out of sequence numbered check for ten-thousand dollars and signed my name. To delay me finding out about it, he stole it from a surplus pad of checks I kept in my desk drawer.

My blood began to boil. I immediately called him at work to confront him.

Unable to deny the evidence, Keith calmly admitted to writing the check. He claimed he did it because we needed the money and promised to pay the loan right back.

When that excuse did not diffuse my fury, he tried to intimidate me with deflection. He argued that I should not have that feature on my checking account if I never intended to use it.

I hung up on him.

It did not matter what excuse he fabricated or what intimidation tactics he used. He had gone too far this time. Nothing he could possibly say could justify the deceit.

With adrenaline from the anger surging through my body, I felt an uncontrollable urge to run away. I cannot explain it. I just had to get out of there.

I refused to let Keith off the hook for what he had done to me. I wanted him to suffer.

I knew he would be completely lost if I vanished leaving no clue. If he could not find me, he could not manipulate and intimidate me or sweet talk me into coming back. He had no more hands to play. Losing the only power he had in his life—the control over me—would drive him insane.

My sister, Karen, lived in San Diego. I decided to fly there and stay with her. As soon as I hung up on Keith, I got on the phone and arranged for a flight leaving in a few hours. Then I quickly packed my bags and left.

As I relaxed on my cross-country flight, relishing in the thought of Keith's misery, all hell had broken loose at home.

Keith had lost his house key that day and came home expecting me to let him in. It angered him that he had to break into the house by climbing in the window.

He had already called my parents and started working on them. I had not told them that I left or where I went for that exact reason. If they knew nothing, he could get nothing out of them.

When I landed in San Diego, I called to let my parents know I was alright.

They told me that Keith had called them sounding very upset. They thought I should call him right away to ease his mind.

I explained what he had done to me and how I planned to punish him for it. They told me I was being too hard on him.

I refused to disclose my location to them until they promised not to tell Keith *anything*.

They reluctantly agreed.

Keith called my parents several times a day and cried to them.

Cliffedge Road

Each day, the messages they passed on to me from him became more and more pitiful. He knew they were a weak link and he could use them to get to me.

My parents felt sorry for Keith and were cracking under his pressure. Every time I called them, they pleaded with me to call him.

It pissed me off that I could not count on their support. Tired of their pathetic whining, I told them I would call and deal with Keith myself. They sounded incredibly relieved to hear that.

Keith slammed me with three days of pent-up anger; so much for the pitiful crying act he had laid on my parents.

He tried to bully me into telling him my location but I refused. He threatened that I had better get home right away or I would not have a home to come back to.

I told him I did not care if I ever came back and then hung up on him.

By the next day, he had changed his approach. He began sweet-talking me and negotiating for my return. For the umpteenth time, he professed his undying love for me. He pleaded that he could not survive without me.

His words weakened my resolve and dissipated my anger, but I refused to let him know that. I did not feel he had suffered long enough.

I told him I might be home in a few days, and then hung up on him.

I called two days later from the payphone at the Baltimore Washington International airport, anticipating an enthusiastic greeting. Instead, I got a bland, indifferent one.

Keith answered the phone with a scratchy sounding voice. He claimed he had been sleeping. I told him I had just landed in Baltimore and would be home soon. He yawned and simply responded, "Okay."

While in sunny Southern California, I had given no thought to the winter weather back home. I only learned of the raging snowstorm that had befallen Baltimore when I stepped outside the airport to get the parking lot shuttle. Sleepy Keith had mentioned nothing about it.

I hopped off the bus carrying my suitcases and trudged to my car through the knee-deep snow wearing sandals.

By the time I cleared the driver's side door and the windshield off, the skin on my hands and feet had turned white and burned so bad I feared I had frostbite.

I sat in the car waiting for the heat to warm me up. Once I felt better, I switched from the heat to the defroster hoping it would clear the windows. But the snow was coming down so hard and fast, it could not keep up with the accumulation.

The drive home did not concern me. I had already switched my regular tires to snow tires in preparation for winter weather and had lots of experience driving in the snow. Everything considered, I decided to hit the road.

I got back out of the car and cleared off as much of the windshield as I could, and then put my wipers on high speed and slowly headed for the highway.

The roads leading out of the airport had not been plowed but I figured the highway would have already been cleared and salted.

As I merged from the ramp onto the highway, I could see that it had not. Tractor-trailers and cars were sliding sideways and skidding all over the place.

Unable to turn back at that point, I shifted my automatic gears into low and began inching along the highway.

I had never seen such treacherous conditions. The rapidly falling snow had reduced visibility to only about one hundred feet.

The snow fell so hard and fast that it covered my windshield faster than the wipers could remove it. All my other windows were covered with snow. Barely able to see where I was going, I just kept inching along the right side of the highway.

Staying on the highway meant imminent danger. I knew of a Howard Johnson's on Route 40 West a few miles away. I hoped to make it that far without incident and then get off the highway and stay the night.

When I finally saw the Howard Johnson's hotel sign from the highway, I breathed a huge sigh of relief. Other drivers had the same idea. I followed a line of cars exiting the highway and turning into the hotel parking lot.

I had not spoken to Keith for three hours. Figuring he would be worried sick about me, I called to update him the minute I got into my room.

After a few rings, he answered the telephone sounding just as lifeless as he had earlier. He claimed, again, that he had been sleeping. He had no awareness of the blizzard raging right outside his door or that three hours had passed since we had last spoken.

Hungering for some kind of consolation, I described the details of my harrowing experience. His feeble attempt to comfort me while yawning only made me feel worse. I told him I would be home tomorrow and then hung up the phone.

I sat down on the bed, crestfallen and lonely. I had gone from euphoric empowerment a few days before to unbearable guilt. Silent tears streamed down my face. I felt painfully unappreciated yet blamed myself for creating the mess. His transgressions seemed to pale in comparison to mine.

I wondered if the "powers that be" had punished me for running away. I believed I had gotten exactly what I deserved.

The Backgammon Game

....

We all learn from experience but some of us have to go through summer school. ~Peter De Vries

....

"Relationships don't just happen. They take work."
I do not know exactly where I heard that advice, but the concept had clung to my psyche like burs to a cotton sock. The statement further evolved in my mind to mean, "Relationships are burdensome and backbreaking. Like war, they are only won with blood, sweat, and tears."

I had taken on this responsibility willingly and with eyes wide open. I did not take that commitment lightly. No matter how hard, I planned to see it through.

It never occurred to me that I had needs or that they were just as important as Keith's. I had no idea I had lost myself in the process of trying to fix him. I believed the problem had nothing to do with me and everything to do with him. Given the right approach, I would ultimately get through to him.

Whatever I had done seemed to have worked; at least I wanted to believe it had.

After returning home from California, our relationship went

into a honeymoon phase. We took a three-day trip to Florida to get away from everything and reconnect with each other.

We had a great time during the day, but Keith fell seriously ill every night. He spent hours in the bathtub sweating out his fever and vomiting from nausea. He thought he might have some kind of virus. It definitely seemed that way.

It never crossed my mind that his suffering had anything to do with withdrawal. I only saw what I wanted to see.

Keith seemed to hold it together for a while after we returned home from Florida—as far as I could tell. Basking in the glory of our drama-free life, I avoided the topic of his sobriety. Though I still kept my eye on him, I stopped worrying as much.

One afternoon in the middle of one of our backgammon games, we heard a knock at the door. Keith got up from the sofa to open the door. He greeted a casual friend standing there, invited him into the house, and then led him back to the kitchen. He assured me he would be right back to finish our game.

A few minutes later, he walked his friend back to the front door and said goodbye. Then he sat back down and we resumed our game.

About fifteen minutes later, I noticed a distinct change in Keith's demeanor. His eyes started looking heavy and his speech slowed down. Within a very short time, he started slurring his speech and his eyelids kept drifting closed. I knew he had taken Quaaludes.

I glared at him through hateful, narrowed eyes. "That guy just came here to sell you Quaaludes, didn't he?"

He incoherently blabbered, as if suddenly struck dumb, "I can't argue with you. You are de–fi—nite—ly right."

"That's it. It's over." I shoved the backgammon board as hard as I could into his stomach and stood up.

"Don't leeeave!" he pleaded.

I darted around the house like a crazed animal, grabbing whatever belonged to me. I took armloads of belongings to my car and then went back inside to get more.

Trying desperately to get to the front door and block it, he tried over and over to stand up, but could not. He cried and pleaded with me not to leave him.

By the time I had finished loading all my belongings into my car, he had somehow managed to get out the front door and crawl down two sets of concrete steps. I found him lying on the sidewalk next to my car crying out, "You caaaan't leeeave me!"

I got in my car, locked the doors, and turned on the engine. I watched in disgust as Keith crawled on his hands and knees off the curb and into the middle of the street behind my car. As I pulled away, I looked in my rear-view mirror and saw him on all fours hopelessly trying to crawl up the street after me. I had never seen a more pitiful sight, but I could not be moved. I had finally reached my saturation point.

I drove to my parents' house only a mile away. They were shocked and troubled to hear about Keith's relapse, though confusingly sympathetic towards his problem. They typically spoke with disdain, disgust, and contempt about anyone whom they even suspected used drugs.

I told them I loved Keith with all my heart, but that his drug addiction and the emotional abuse attached to it was tearing me apart. I explained how difficult it had been to leave him but that I had no choice—if I didn't leave, he would surely destroy me.

I stressed how hard it would be for me to hear his voice—that the mere sound of it would have me running right back to him. I pleaded with them to support me in my decision.

Having poured out my heart about the hell Keith had put me through; I begged them not to put his calls through to me under any circumstance.

They agreed and promised to support me in whatever I needed them to do.

With my father's help, I unloaded my car and brought all my belongings into their house. Once we had emptied the car, I went upstairs to my old bedroom, sprawled out on the bed, and fell to pieces.

After sobering up hours later, Keith began calling. My father fielded the calls for me each time. But I could tell by his annoyingly compassionate tone that he could not keep it up for very long. That angered me. My outspoken father did not talk that way to *anyone*.

Keith confessed all his wrong-doings to my parents and pleaded for their forgiveness. They bought his sob story hook, line, and sinker. After only two days, they were pressing me to take his calls.

Sitting with my father in the kitchen one morning, the telephone rang. I could tell by the tone of his voice that he had Keith on the other end. He looked at me with pleading eyes, and pointed to the receiver.

I sternly glared at him and motioned impatiently for him to hand me the receiver. He somberly said, "Hold on, Keith, I'll let you talk to her."

I knew I was a goner before he even spoke to me.

"Hi, Baby. I am so sorry for all the pain I have caused you. I have not stopped crying since you left me. I love you more than I have ever loved anything or anyone. I cannot live without you. Please come back to me. Tell me what I need to do. I'll do whatever you say. Just please come back."

I stated the conditions of my return. He promised to do whatever it took to keep me in his life.

And just like that, I packed up my things and went back to him—again.

Keith's Red Shoes

....

The trouble with some women is that they get all excited about nothing—and then marry him. ~Cher

....

Keith immediately started seeing an addiction therapist and began religiously attending NA meetings. He made tremendous progress with those support systems behind him.

I occasionally met with the therapist to get progress reports. He felt that Keith had been doing everything he needed to do to stay clean, which included working his Narcotics Anonymous twelve-step program.

I felt proud and very relieved that he had kept up his end of the bargain. He soon chalked up five months of sobriety. It seemed as if I finally had the old Keith back.

It felt as if a huge weight had been lifted off my shoulders. With the knowledge that he had a support team other than me in place, I could finally relax.

Our relationship began to strengthen and move in a positive direction. We looked forward to spending our lives together.

Don't get me wrong, I knew that anything could trigger a relapse. But I had to remain positive, looking only toward the future, not dwelling on the past. Reliving those nightmares only depressed and exhausted me. That did not benefit either of us.

We had met in the spring of 1981 and we were now in the spring of 1982. As I am recalling the story, I find it incredulous that so much had transpired in just twelve months. At the time, it seemed like an eternity. Somehow, our relationship had survived and we made it to our one-year anniversary.

To celebrate our milestone, Keith took me to The Prime Rib—one of the finest restaurants in town, notorious for their excellent food and superior service.

After a scrumptious dinner, as we waited for our desserts, Keith dropped down on one knee and proposed to me. He placed a beautiful diamond engagement ring on my finger.

Certain that the marriage proposal represented his good-faith commitment to stay straight, I said yes without hesitation.

My love, devotion, and understanding had finally fixed him. It *was* true—love *did* conquer all.

I shared the good news with my family who I knew would enthusiastically support our engagement. Having already chosen to overlook Keith's troubled past, my parents happily welcomed him and his parents into our family.

When I met with Keith's mother to share the news, she went on the offensive. I will never forget her icy admonishment.

She asked me why I wanted to marry her son. I told her I loved him very much and wanted to spend my life with him.

She snapped, "Marry him and believe me, your love for him will turn to hate."

Right or wrong, I wondered how a mother could say such a hurtful, vicious thing about her own son. I just ignored her. If she didn't support the marriage, so be it.

Keith and I decided on November 28th of the same year, 1982, for our wedding date. That gave me six months to plan it.

He left all the wedding details up to me, except for one. He obstinately maintained that neither he nor his parents would be walking down the aisle. That being his second marriage, they thought it hypocritical.

The self-centeredness of his mandate really stung. I did not need a fancy bridal procession but I would have at least liked my groom to walk down the aisle and wait for me.

I knew better than to fight about it. When he made up his bullheaded mind, he would not yield an inch.

With or without Keith, this bride planned to walk down the aisle.

Keith's family had no affiliation with a synagogue, therefore, did not have a rabbi to marry us. My parents had a rabbi, but I felt no personal connection to him.

I had heard of a young, progressive-minded rabbi in town whose congregation adored him. He sounded like a good fit for us. I called his office and scheduled an appointment to meet with him.

I first met with the rabbi alone. Then he asked to meet with us as a couple so he could get to know us better and offer some marriage counseling.

Keith and I sat together on the sofa in the rabbi's chambers while he discussed the responsibilities of a Jewish husband and wife. To get a sense of our personalities and the dynamics of our relationship, he asked us both some questions.

I can still picture the perturbed look on the rabbi's face after hearing some of Keith's responses. I cannot remember the exact questions asked of him or specifically how Keith replied. I only recall the rabbi looking at me before we left, shaking his head from side to side, and sarcastically saying, "Good luck!"

We decided on Hawaii as our honeymoon destination. Neither of us had ever been there and we both looked forward to going.

I asked Keith if we had a honeymoon budget. He told me not to worry about that. Money would not be an issue.

We met with a travel agent and arranged to stay in the best hotels on Oahu, Maui, and the big island of Hawaii…the grand total of the trip—cha-ching—five thousand dollars. Keith did not flinch.

I bought a silvery-gray dress trimmed in red and black to wear as my "going away outfit", and found black patent leather shoes trimmed with red piping that matched.

When Keith saw my dress, he decided to match the colors of his outfit to mine. He bought red leather loafers to go with it.

Six months quickly passed while I busied myself with the wedding planning. Before I knew it, November had arrived.

The rabbi, though not a great fan of Keith, conducted a beautiful ceremony for us.

In preparation for our first dance, we had taken lessons and learned to Foxtrot. When the band announced us into the reception room as Mr. and Mrs. we took the floor and danced to our song "All The Way".

We must have looked ridiculous dancing around the floor so stiff and proper, but we felt good about our accomplishment.

As the reception came to a close, Keith and I slipped out of the room to change into our matching "going away" outfits. Then we re-entered the reception hall to surprise our guests.

Everyone started laughing and pointing to Keith's feet. He totally upstaged me with his red shoes. I did not mind him stealing the limelight. Keith's signature style was one of the things I loved best about him.

When the wedding reception ended, we counted all the money we had received as gifts, and then I handed all the envelopes to my father to take home for us. He gathered up our gifts and any miscellaneous clothing to safeguard until we returned from our honeymoon.

We got into the limo awaiting us at the front door, posed for a few last pictures, and then waved goodbye and rode happily off into the sunset.

No Turning Back

....

The difficulty with marriage is that we fall in love with a personality, but must live with a character. ~Peter Devries

....

On the Monday morning following our wedding, we boarded the 747-jet airplane that would fly us across the country. After a brief scheduled layover in Los Angeles, we boarded the second plane that would take us to our first destination—Oahu, Hawaii.

Caught up in newlywed rapture, strapped into our unyielding airline seats, we reminisced about our wedding day. Our guests had been more than generous with their monetary gifts. I looked forward to depositing the considerable sum of money in the joint bank account I planned to open when we got back home.

Keith and I had never discussed our financial plans but that was not unusual. He made the money, I paid the bills.

When I brought up the savings account, he looked at me as if I were crazy. He told me in his stubborn, authoritative tone that there would be no money to start a bank account; we needed all the gift money to pay for our honeymoon.

Words cannot describe how shocked and devastated I felt.

I asked him why he never mentioned using our wedding money during the planning of our "spare no expense" honeymoon.

He deflected it right back at me. He asked me where I expected the money to come from; as if I were being greedy and should have known.

I consoled myself with the possibility that I might have made incorrect assumptions about the money. Maybe I did sound greedy.

I couldn't dwell on it. We were married now and on our honeymoon. I had no choice but to let it go.

After twelve hours of traveling, we arrived on the island of Oahu, both of us exhausted from the long flight.

We rented a car at the airport and took a short drive around Honolulu to get our bearings before going to our hotel, The Hilton Hawaiian Village Beach Resort, to settle in.

To commemorate the first night of our honeymoon, we asked the hotel Concierge to book us an eight o'clock reservation at the best restaurant on the island. Then we went to our room and rested for a few hours.

The Concierge selected a tranquil, elegant five-star restaurant. I ordered the seafood special of the night; jumbo prawns. Keith had Prime Rib and shared some of my prawns.

After dinner, exhausted from the long trip, we went back to our hotel looking forward to a rejuvenating sleep followed by an exciting next day exploring the island.

I awoke suddenly at two a.m. to a loud retching sound. I looked next to me and Keith was not in bed.

I got out of bed and found him in the bathroom. I had never seen him so deathly ill, violently vomiting, clutching his stomach, and grimacing in pain.

As I helplessly stood by looking on, the same syndrome overtook me; first nausea and acute stomach pains, then uncontrollable vomiting and diarrhea.

We were a horrendous sight; one toilet and two waist-baskets between us, both violently erupting from both ends.

The agonizing purge continued uninterrupted for hours. When it finally stopped, we both collapsed in bed. Every bone in our bodies ached. The gripping stomach spasms still would not let up.

We clearly had food poisoning. We could only deduce that the prawns, the only food we had both eaten, were the culprits.

As we thought about what could have happened, we remembered hearing about the monstrous hurricane that had hit the Hawaiian Islands days before we arrived. The island of Kauai had been devastated but Oahu suffered very little damage. Related or not, somehow, the prawns had gotten contaminated.

Certain we were not the only diners at the "five-star" restaurant who were poisoned by the bad seafood, we waited a few hours for the restaurant to open and then called them.

The restaurant manager adamantly denied receiving any other complaints. We had no way to prove our allegation.

I kiddingly commented to Keith that I hoped the food poisoning was not a bad omen. Though it hurt our stomachs to do so, we both laughed.

After three days of recuperation in the hotel room, we both felt better. Unfortunately, we had spent our entire visit on Oahu sick in bed.

Next on our itinerary: two days on the awe-inspiring big island of Hawaii. We spent the final two days of our honeymoon at the Hyatt resort in Lahaina, Maui—a perfect conclusion to our "dream vacation".

A Woman's Touch

....

What screws us up most in life is the picture in our head of how it is supposed to be. -Jeremy Binns

....

After returning from our Hawaiian honeymoon, we began life as newlyweds. I continued working my part-time office job and Keith resumed his usual work schedule.

Keith had stopped attending Narcotic Anonymous meetings and did have an occasional drink, but all things considered, he seemed okay.

I could not stand to look at the dilapidated bachelor pad anymore. As a wedding present, Keith's parents offered to pay for new living room furniture, some cosmetic renovations, and a full kitchen remodel.

I had the shag carpet removed from the walls of one of the upstairs dormers and the black ceiling repainted, and then moved our bedroom up there. The formerly atrocious space became a cozy little sanctum.

The room that had previously served as our bedroom/hodgepodge room became a comfy den, which became our hangout room.

I hired a glass company to remove the hideous gold marbleized mirror squares in the living room and recover the entire wall with a solid mirror.

I ordered a cheerful sectional sofa with lots of loose pillows, and an oriental-style brass coffee table for the living room. We sold the homely brown sofa and put the old busted up coffee table out to pasture.

The entire interior got a fresh coat of paint or wallpaper, and I had new blinds installed on all the windows.

I had a beautiful, new custom-designed kitchen installed.

The stale outdated bachelor-pad finally had a woman's touch. Now it felt like home. I looked forward to Keith making it official by adding my name to the title of the house.

Months went by as I patiently waited for Keith to bring the subject up, but he never did. I got tired of waiting so I just came out and asked him.

"Now that we're married, when will you be adding my name to the title of the house?"

He looked at me and arrogantly replied, "Never."

Unsure I heard him right, I repeated the word back to him. "Did you say, never?"

He reaffirmed his answer. "That's right—never."

I resorted to tears hoping it would at least make him consider my feelings. But he would have none of it.

After suffering so many disappointments with him, I had conditioned myself to be grateful for small favors. At least he had let me fix up the house exactly the way I wanted to. I hoped in time he would reconsider adding my name to the title.

A few weeks after that episode, I suppose as a consolation, he offered to buy me a new car. I had still been driving the 1969 Pontiac Lemans my parents had given me. That definitely took the sting out of the house title rejection.

I custom ordered a luxurious white Pontiac Grand Prix Brougham Coupe with a lush navy-blue velour interior, outfitted with all the bells and whistles. It was the first new car I had ever owned. He put the title entirely in my name. I felt like a million bucks driving it.

We decided to hold on to the Lemans. With low mileage and in beautiful condition, it would soon be a collector's car.

Since we did not have a garage at our house, Keith thought it safest to park it behind the produce stand on their private property.

The Lemans had only been parked there for a few months when the Parkville Police Department called our house asking if I owned the car. At first, I thought they might have had a problem with the expired registration.

They told me that someone had reported my car parked in front of their house and if I did not move it that day, they would have to impound it.

Keith and I grabbed the keys to the Lemans and drove his car to the specified location. Keith planned to drive the Lemans back to the produce stand while I followed in his car.

The Lemans had been abandoned on a residential side street no more than a mile from the produce stand. Keith pulled behind the car and parked. From where I sat in the passenger seat, I could see no visible signs of damage.

Keith got out of his car. I slid over to the driver's side ready to follow him.

He walked over to the Lemans, unlocked the driver-side door, and opened it. Then he looked back at me and motioned for me to come to him.

I could hardly believe what I saw. We both stood aghast, bent over and peering in through the open door. It was a desolate wasteland. The vandal had stolen all the seats, the steering wheel, and the audio equipment.

The senseless savage destruction of such a well-kept classic car; the one I had relied on for so many years, upset me.

I felt so sad watching the tow truck take her away. She did not deserve such an unfortunate fate.

Looking back, I am certain Keith had something to do with it.

Unrelenting Drama

....

Expect trouble as an inevitable part of life and repeat to yourself the most comforting words of all; this too shall pass ~Ann Landers

....

I had assumed that life with "Sober Keith" meant life devoid of drama. I could not have been more wrong. The pattern of crazy situations, one after another, continued without pause.

Some bizarre predicament, seemingly out of the blue, would kick me in the ass and elevate my stress level. I just could not get any traction in my predictably unpredictable drama-laden life.

Keith instigated most of the problems that arose in my life, but not all of them. A few were just casualties of life, augmented by my ignorance or naivety.

The Cliffedge Road house had its share of age-related problems. The fact that Keith took no preventative measures nor maintained it in any way did not help.

The house had a "French drain", a three-inch-wide trench between the cinder-block walls and the concrete foundation around the entire perimeter of the basement floor. In the event of a flood, the water would run through the gravel-filled trench and then out through the perforated pipe at the bottom.

The antiquated drain had probably served the house well for many years. But since Keith had not cleaned or serviced it in years, the drain had become clogged with tree roots and debris.

I had packed all my sentimental keepsakes: cards, letters, memory books, photo albums, year-books, etc. in boxes before I moved out of my parents' house, and then took the boxes with me each time I moved.

When I moved into the Cliffedge Road house, I stored the boxes on the floor of the basement.

I could have just as easily put the boxes on tables or shelves, but since I had never lived in a house with a basement, the flooding potential never crossed my mind—and Keith never warned me.

The basement flooded but I did not discover the standing water until a few days later when I went down there to do laundry. By then, the soaked boxes had disintegrated and all my treasured, irreplaceable books and papers were unsalvageable. The memorabilia I had treasured and saved my entire life all had to be thrown away.

…and the chaos continued.

Early one evening, Keith came home from work. It had started to snow but not heavily yet. He walked through the door holding a zippered bank bag with the days' receipts from the produce market. That seemed unusual. I had never seen him bring money from work home before.

He took off his shoes at the front door and then went straight back to the den to place the bag on the coffee table.

The news forecast predicted a significant amount of snow accumulation. I thought it would be wise to make a grocery run before being holed up for any length of time. So, we quickly bundled up, locked up the house, and drove the two-mile stretch to the grocery store. We were there and back within thirty minutes.

The dogs enthusiastically greeted us when we walked in through the door. Dusted from head to toe with snow, we dropped our damp jackets on the floor, kicked off our shoes, and headed to the kitchen with our packages.

After I put my package on the counter, I noticed out of the corner of my eye that the doormat had been moved. That seemed odd because I would have never left it like that, so I bent down to straighten it. As I slid it closer to the door, I uncovered a mass of shattered glass hidden underneath it.

I asked Keith if he knew anything about the broken glass. He looked at me puzzled and then bent down beside me to get a closer look. Then he stood back up and raised the mini blinds to check the back-door window. Sure enough, the glass directly over the deadbolt key had been busted out.

We started walking from room to room to see what the burglar had taken. Everything looked exactly as it had thirty minutes prior. My purse which I had not taken with me hadn't been stolen or ransacked. My jewelry had not been touched or stolen either. Only one thing was missing—the bank bag holding all the cash.

Since Keith never brought cash home from work, it seemed unlikely he could have been followed. The robbery, way too coincidental to be random, too well planned to be spontaneous, looked like a set-up.

Every road pointed to Keith's involvement, though I couldn't imagine when he could have possibly planned it. He had no idea I would ask him to take me to the grocery store. I did not see him call anyone before we left. And it all went down in thirty minutes.

When Keith told his father what had happened to the money, he blew a fuse. He did not buy Keith's story at all.

Keith adamantly denied he had anything to do with the break-in and robbery. He acted as if he felt hurt by the accusation. I dutifully defended him.

The crime never got solved, but I am sure Keith had arranged it. To this day, I have not figured out exactly how he pulled it off.

…And then the degenerate thug showed up.

Not long after the bank bag incident, Keith learned that his brother Mike would soon be released from prison. Keith felt sorry

Cliffedge Road

for Mike because he had nowhere to go and asked me if he could live with us for a while.

I told him, "absolutely not." The thought of being alone in the house with that criminal frightened me. He had been in and out of prison for years. I had no idea what he might do.

The drug issue worried me even more. I had worked so hard to keep Keith off of drugs and away from temptation. Nothing good could come from having Mike around.

I told Keith I could not tolerate having an ex-con, brother or no brother, living in our house. Keith promised his brother's stay would be very temporary, only long enough to find his own place. After that, his parents would take the responsibility.

He pressured me until I consented, albeit reluctantly.

As it turned out, I had nothing to be afraid of. Mike looked creepy and could be trusted for nothing, but I found him generally harmless. Still, I did not like having him around.

I can recall one incident that particularly demonstrated his unsavory character.

One evening, the three of us went to a video rental store. As Keith and I stood facing the shelf of videotapes, Mike tapped me on the shoulder and motioned for me to turn around.

After getting my attention, he pointed to a blonde-haired teenage boy standing on the other side of the store. Then he started making kissing noises and thrusting his hips in the boy's direction.

Fortunately, the boy didn't notice Mike's perverted gestures. I did not give him the satisfaction of a reaction because I knew he had done that to get a rise out of me.

As far as I knew, Mike identified as a heterosexual male. Years in prison might have altered his orientation. More likely, he just wanted to impress me with his "bad-ass" prison behavior. He did not succeed. I found his behavior utterly repulsive.

I do have to give it to Keith, he really worked hard at finding his brother a new place. In less than a month, we were rid of him.

The Double Whammy

....

*I don't know what's worst, being taken for granted
or being played like a fool. ~Unknown*

....

Keith's mother extended an invitation for me and my mother to come to Boca Raton, Florida, and stay in her spare condo. My mother and I had never vacationed together. I looked forward to watching her experience the luxurious "Boca life" the way I had.

My in-laws lived in a villa apartment on the grounds of the Boca Raton Hotel. In addition to that, they had recently purchased a two-bedroom oceanfront condo in a luxurious high-rise building nearby. That is where my mother and I stayed.

Each day, the three of us went to The Boca Beach Club. My father-in-law slept during the day so he didn't join us until dinner time.

Every evening, they wined and dined us at a different restaurant. We were treated royally.

On the third evening of our Florida trip, Keith's aunt and uncle joined us for dinner at an Italian restaurant. I sat between my mother and my mother-in-law at a round table.

My scotch-sloshed mother-in-law started bragging to me about

Cliffedge Road

how much she loved living in Florida. I commented that I loved Florida too and hoped to live there someday.

My innocuous remark triggered the crazy in her. She flew into a rage and started yelling so loudly at me, everyone in the restaurant turned to look at us. "Your place is at home with your husband, not here in Florida. He's got a business to run there and that's your home!"

Humiliated by her outburst, I stood up and ran out of the restaurant. My mother followed after me, all-the-while imploring that I ignore my mother-in-law's drunken tantrum. I could not. Drunk or not, she had no right to treat me that way.

I found the nearest payphone and called Keith to tell him what his mother had just done. He offered the same advice my mother had: she was drunk and I should just ignore her.

It's pretty hard to ignore someone vociferously raging at you. I had seen her drunk many times but she had never gone off on me like that.

I asked Keith if he thought I should fly home early. He suggested I do whatever felt right to me. If I wanted to come home early, I should.

Then he said, "There is no easy way to tell you what I have to tell you. I feel terrible that I have to break such bad news to you when you already feel the way you do. I intended to wait until you came home from your vacation, but since you might come home early, I should probably tell you now."

My breath seized. I braced myself for the worst possible news. If Keith considered it bad, it had to be monstrously horrible.

He went on to explain that while driving my Grand Prix, he had "accidentally" hit a mass transit bus. He had not gotten hurt but my car was severely damaged.

The news shocked and outraged me. I could not believe that my rat-bastard of a husband had gotten loaded and wrecked my beautiful brand-new car. He should not have been driving it in the first place. He knew he was not allowed to.

Keith apologized for what he had done but I refused to accept it. I only wanted to know where they had taken my car and when I would get it back.

He told me my car had been towed to our friend Bruce's car repair body shop and it would take three to four weeks to fix it.

I found a tiny bit of consolation knowing that Bruce would give us preferential treatment.

Keith swore that in a few weeks my car would be good as new. I told him it better be and hung up on him

I sat down on the curb, put my head in my hands, and burst into tears. I felt totally defeated. I had not fully processed the shock of what Keith had done and still had to contend with the bitterness I felt towards my mother-in-law.

For the rest of the evening and the entire next day, I did not look at her or talk to her. I wanted her to know how much she had angered me.

She never mentioned the incident or apologized for it. My mother acted as if nothing had happened too—textbook narcissistic behavior from both of them.

For the remainder of the vacation, Keith's mother bent over backwards to make me happy. And to avoid causing a huge rift between us, I decided not to shorten my trip. My mother and I returned home at the originally scheduled time.

Keith had promised my car would be fixed and returned to me in three to four weeks, but that did not happen.

At the end of the four weeks, I asked him why I did not have my car back yet. He claimed that the insurance settlement had taken longer than expected, so Bruce had been unable to order the parts he needed to repair it. Though disappointed, I gave him the benefit of the doubt. He had given me a somewhat plausible explanation.

With every passing week that I did not have my car, I got angrier and more frustrated. Keith kept asking me to be patient. He assured me he had everything handled.

I tried to be patient, but two months went by, then three, then four, and still no car.

I confronted Keith again. He remarked, sounding equally frustrated, that he could not imagine why Bruce had not finished fixing my car yet.

If Keith had "handled" things the way he claimed he had, I would have already had my car back. Fed up with his incompetent management of the situation, I stopped waiting and took over control. Bruce and I were about to have a serious confrontation.

I paid an impromptu visit to Bruce at his body shop, and then asked him to step outside so I could speak with him.

Fed up after months of being run around, I launched into a tirade of accusations.

Bruce stood there calmly waiting for me to finish. Then with a smirk on his face, he said, "I'm not the person you should be angry with. If you want to be angry with anyone, it should be your husband."

I asked him what he meant by that.

He claimed that Keith had taken the entire insurance settlement and cashed it in. He had not fixed my car because he did not have enough money to do so.

I stood there dumbfounded. I felt so foolish for attacking Bruce the way I had, though I knew he wasn't as innocent as he pretended to be. The two of them were probably in cahoots.

I wanted my car returned to me in its original condition and refused to wait any longer. Come hell or high water, Keith had better make that happen.

When I confronted Keith with Bruce's allegation, he admitted to taking some of the insurance money. He lied, just as he did every time he got caught, and maintained that we needed the money to pay bills.

Then he tried to deflect the blame away from him and put it back on Bruce. He contended that he had given Bruce more than enough money to fix the car, and suggested that Bruce had put it "all up his nose".

I didn't believe either one of them. I knew they were both trying to play me.

From that day forward, I put so much pressure on both of them, neither one could wait to get rid of me. And what do you know? Within two weeks, I had my car back.

The car looked good as new. Unfortunately, some of my favorite bells and whistles never worked again.

From that day forward, I kept my car keys hidden from Keith.

Randi in front of childhood home 2 years old (1960)

Randi's childhood home

Randi singing and playing guitar 6 years old (1964)

Randi singing and playing guitar at talent show 14 years old (1972)

Randi with Shane, the dog Greg bought her for protection

Keith's yellow Lincoln Continental

Cliffedge Road house

Mike left (brother), Keith right (1970)

Keith with his grandmother (1980)

Randi and Keith on wedding day (1982)

Randi and Keith in wedding day "going away" outfits featuring Keith's red shoes (1982)

Jan 31, 1985

This morning I am consumed with worry and projection. I need to realize what I have to be thankful for.

I am thankful that:
   I am alive
   Keith is alive
   We are both healthy
   My family is healthy
   We have a warm house to shelter us
   We have food to eat
   There is a NA and Nar-Anon Program

That's a lot to be thankful for. I have no right to expect more. I asked my higher power to help me with surrender. I just don't seem to be able to do it alone. I asked my higher power to watch over Keith. Somehow I keep thinking that I can watch over him. That's impossible. I pray for help today.

Randi's journal entry (1985)

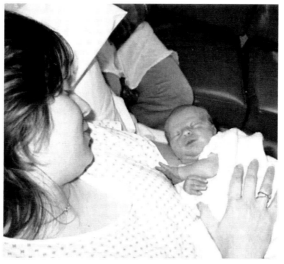
Randi with newborn Cammy (1985)

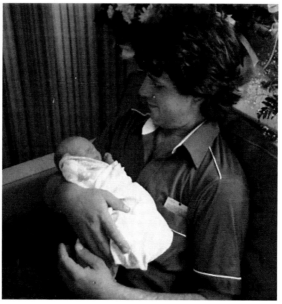
Keith with newborn Cammy (1985)

Keith visiting Cammy after our separation (1985)

Keith's last letter to me from the hospital (1987)

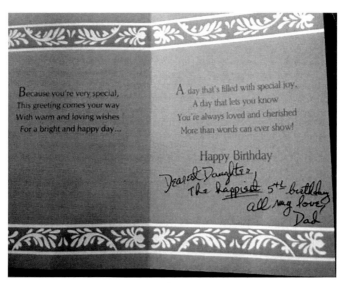

Keith's last birthday card to Cammy (1990)

Cammy and Billy (1987)

Billy and Cammy at Boca Raton Beach Club (1988)

Randi, Cammy, Billy (1988)

"Engagement ring" Billy gave Cammy (1988)

Randi and Billy wedding day (1988)

Randi, Cammy, Billy, wedding day (1988)

"Velvet Hills South" house Randi and Billy built (1989)

Cammy with teddy bear "Violet" (1989)

Baby Fever

....

*Even miracles take a little time. ~Fairy
Godmother (Cinderella)*

....

I know. No woman in her right mind would have stayed in such a horrible marriage or put up with so much outrage. I was not in my right mind.

Years of childhood narcissistic abuse conditioning had skewed my perception of reality, especially as it related to adult relationships. I thought I knew what love looked like and felt like, but in truth, I did not have a clue.

I didn't love or respect myself either. My worth depended entirely on how others defined it, and on how well I could fix and please people.

The belief that marriage is a difficult undertaking kept replaying in my head. No wonder; I had observed the dysfunctional dynamic of my parents' relationship for years. I knew no other way to love or be loved.

I clung to the hope that everything would get better with persistence and time. I would make that marriage work, even if it took a lifetime. Unless it killed me first, I would find some way to fix Keith.

Love would conquer all. It just had to.

Now twenty-five, I longed to become a mother. Keith had always dreamed of being a father. We talked it over and decided we were ready to start our family.

I agree that on paper the decision to have a baby with Keith sounds grossly irresponsible. But I did not see it that way. Though painful, confusing, and frustrating, the life I had with him felt normal to me. I had never lived any other way. Saying that my life felt "normal" does not mean I enjoyed living that way. I did not.

Keith made my life miserable. I loathed his drug addiction. I despised the hurtful things he did to me. I found his stubbornness exasperating. I couldn't trust him as far as I could throw him. There were times I wanted to kill him. But I loved the man more than life itself. I believed I could not live without him.

Before trying to conceive, I talked to my OB/GYN about the effect Keith's drug abuse might have on a developing fetus. He told me there were no studies showing that the father's drug abuse had any effect on the baby.

He did recommend we have genetic testing done for Tay-Sachs. Jewish people of *Ashkenazi* descent, which we both were, have a higher than average risk of passing the fatal disease on to their children.

Tay-Sachs damages the nerve and brain cells of the child. If both parents are carriers there is a chance that any child they have will be born with the disease.

We definitely wanted to rule that out. My doctor recommended a lab that screened for it. I called and scheduled an appointment for both of us to get tested.

Keith sat in the room with me while the phlebotomist drew my blood. I planned on doing the same with him. But when it was his turn, he asked me to wait outside the room. I looked at him puzzled. He told me he would explain later.

Keith apologized to me afterwards. He explained that after having shot up for so many years, most of the veins in his arms had collapsed. The easiest veins to draw blood from were in his ankles. He claimed he did not want me to have to see that.

In retrospect, I believe he probably had fresh track marks up and down his arms that he did not want me to see. At the time, that thought never crossed my mind.

When we received the test results, we were relieved to find out that neither of us carried the gene. With that concern out of the way, we began trying to conceive a baby.

Conception did not occur as fast as we expected it to. Month after month we hoped for my pregnancy but ended up disappointed.

After six months of unsuccessful attempts, I consulted my OB/GYN. He told me not to worry; it could take up to a year to conceive.

When I reached my eleventh month without success, I purchased a Basal Thermometer and started charting the temperature changes in my ovulation cycle. The body temperature rises during a woman's most fertile time of the month. If conception does not occur, her temperature drops back down until her next ovulation.

After a few mornings of charting my body temperatures, I saw a noticeable rise. It stayed that way for seven days. I also noticed some changes in my body. I called my doctor and he ordered a blood test.

The results came back positive. Pregnant at last and due in early June! We were elated.

The first few weeks of pregnancy went well. I did not suffer any morning sickness. Then between my third and fourth week, the worst nausea I had ever experienced took me over. The sick feeling never eased up. No matter what I tried, I could not get any relief.

Then a disabling fatigue overtook me. I could not lift my head up off the pillow. I just laid in bed, day after day, moaning and bargaining with God.

My sense of smell had dramatically heightened. Subtle odors I had never noticed before now turned me green.

Keith had always been a heavy cigarette smoker. I never minded the smell on him before. Now I found the odor that clung to him repulsive.

Each day when he came home from work, I could smell the vegetables he had trimmed up. I could also smell what stores he had delivered produce to. I could not stand to have him near me until he took a shower and changed his clothes.

I had never imagined pregnancy would cause me so much suffering. My doctor assured me that my symptoms indicated a healthy pregnancy, so I dealt with the torture one day at a time. Each day, I hoped that tomorrow would be better and tried to focus on the wonderful prize at the end.

Magically, in my fourteenth week, the symptoms disappeared. Suddenly, I felt great. Food smelled and tasted good again, and I had a voracious appetite.

Keith could not wait for me to have the baby. He had dreamed about being a father for as long as he could remember.

I did not want to know the sex of the baby ahead of time and Keith had no reason to find out. He "knew" we were having a girl. Years before, he had chosen the name Cammy for his daughter. He told me that on our first date. I loved the name too.

We had a hard time deciding on a boy's name—a back-up *if* Keith happened to be wrong.

The Man-Cave Charade

....

Optimism is a cheerful frame of mind that enables a tea kettle to sing though it's in hot water up to its nose. ~Author Unknown

....

Keith had tried his best to stay downstairs most of the time to avoid aggravating my symptoms. In his spare time, he began "fixing up" the basement. That seemed strange to me because Keith never fixed or did anything in the house.

Once I felt better, he took me down there, proud to show me his accomplishment. He had moved some things around and brought a television down there. I had never seen him so ambitious. It seemed as if his impending fatherhood had given him a new lease on life.

While confined to bed upstairs and consumed with how badly I felt, Keith had free reign of the downstairs. He could do whatever he wanted without me knowing about it.

I had no idea how often Mike had been coming over and how much time they'd been spending in the basement together. That would have never happened on my watch.

Mike did not care about Keith's best interests. He had always envied him. Now with the baby coming, he had even more reason to sabotage his happiness.

I told Keith I did not like having Mike at our house and did not want him coming over anymore. He said that Mike felt lonely and needed the friendship. I knew nothing positive could come from their companionship.

Unfortunately, by the time I put a stop to their nefarious liaison, the damage had already been done.

Keith never did drugs around me and usually managed to hide his addiction pretty well. Too far gone this time, he could not hide it anymore. I started noticing some signs.

He began giving me less and less money each week to pay the household expenses. The bills had begun to pile up and creditors had started calling.

Keith had always been at work when I called in the morning. Now, every time I called, they told me he was out delivering orders. He would be gone for abnormally long periods of time and return home later than usual.

Keith had become very irresponsible. He lost his house keys at least every other day—sometimes daily. And every morning I found coffee spilled all over the front door.

A strange Mrs. So and So called the house one day asking for Keith. It sounded drug-related and very suspicious.

One Saturday afternoon, Keith asked to borrow my Grand Prix to run an errand. He promised to be extra careful with it and bring it back with a full tank of gas. I reluctantly gave him permission.

Reflecting back, the decision I made astounds me. It's hard to understand how such an irrational decision seemed reasonable to me at the time. It perfectly exemplifies the degree of denial I lived in.

Keith had not been gone thirty minutes before a county police officer called the house asking for me. He had already gotten himself into serious trouble.

The officer explained that while he and his partner were patrolling the area around the nearby middle school, they noticed a suspicious-looking car sitting in what should have been an empty parking lot.

As they approached the car, they saw a man in the driver's seat with a hypodermic needle in his arm. When they asked for his driver's license, he told them he had no identification with him. But he did give the officers his name and explained that his wife owned the car.

I told the officer I would be there in a few minutes.

In the meantime, they ran a background check and discovered that Keith had a revoked license.

When I arrived, my glassy-eyed, stupefied husband peered up at me from the driver's seat. He tried to say something to me but could only mumble. I have no idea what he wanted to tell me. I think he tried to apologize. No matter. No apology would suffice anyway.

The officers showed me everything they had confiscated from my car. They were charging Keith with possession of cocaine, drug paraphernalia, and driving with a revoked license.

They handed me a citation and gave me the option of having him arrested or accepting his release to my custody.

Though tempted to tell the officers to cart Keith off to jail, I believed that decision would only complicate my life. I agreed to take him home.

I did not need my husband sitting in jail. We were going to have a baby and I had to whip him into shape in a hurry.

At the Eleventh Hour

....

Being a drug addict isn't nearly as bad as being sober and loving a drug addict. You can't save them but they can sure as hell destroy you, and they will. ~Unknown

....

Keith had descended into the perilous throes of his most deadly addiction ever—main-line cocaine.

He still tried to hide his dirty little secret from me. I only learned the horrific details when he confessed them to me months later.

Every afternoon, he would leave the produce market under the guise of making deliveries and then head downtown to cop drugs. He often found himself on the wrong side of the barrel of some hoodlum's gun. Amazingly, he never got shot or killed.

After buying the drugs, he got back in his pickup truck, shot up, and then nodded out on the steering wheel for a couple of hours. When he woke up from his drug stupor, he went back to work as if nothing had happened. Then he came home to me at the usual time; sometimes later.

Though I did not know those disturbing details at the time, I could not ignore Keith's rapid decline. I blamed myself for not watching him closely enough.

The eleventh hour had come. The crisis had reached desperate proportions. I had one last chance to save him for the sake of the baby and the future of our family.

If he did not get to inpatient treatment right away, death or incarceration were imminent. Oh, and yes—my safety and wellbeing were seriously at risk too.

I scheduled an emergency appointment for the two of us to see his addiction therapist. It had been months since his last counseling session. I prayed his therapist could persuade him to go to rehab.

It upset but did not surprise me when Keith refused to go. Impossible Keith would not make this process easy for me. He never made anything easy.

As a codependent and enabler, I had spent most of our relationship covering up for him. I had voluntarily assumed that weighty, exhaustive burden. But I could not handle it by myself any longer. I needed his father's help.

Keith's father adored him. He wanted so badly to believe in his son. But after the torment Keith had put his parents through over the years, his father had lost trust.

Since I had protected him from the truth, the news of his son's backslide into addiction would surely devastate him.

I braced myself for the pent-up anger and hollow threats about to be unleashed at me. Though hard to take, I knew that no matter what Keith did, his father would not give up on him.

My father-in-law initially reacted as I expected he would but calmed down quickly and allowed me to explain.

I told him we had to get Keith into treatment immediately and I needed his help to do that.

He asked why I believed rehab would work this time since Keith had gone through it before and relapsed.

I expressed my hope that Keith's dream of becoming a father might possibly give him the motivation to get and stay straight; that for the baby's sake, we had to give rehab a try. We had no other options left.

His father agreed that we should give it a try and asked what I wanted him to do.

I told him to confront Keith about his cocaine addiction, and then tell him he is restricted from coming to work until he goes into treatment.

He did exactly what I asked him to do. When confronted with his addiction, Keith reacted in his usual way. First, he lied about using and denied he had a problem. When that strategy failed, he began pleading his case and begging for compassion. And when that got him nowhere, he began negotiating with his father.

None of his usual tactics worked. His father had backed him into a corner. He had no choice but to concede. He finally agreed to go into treatment.

My father-in-law called me with the good news and then I called Keith's therapist.

His therapist told me about a facility in Lancaster, Pennsylvania called The Terraces that he wanted to send Keith to. He said he would call and make all the arrangements.

He forewarned me that Keith might call me the first night trying to convince me to take him home, but to ignore his excuses. He would just be panicking, as all inpatient addicts do when they realize they cannot get the fix they need.

Everything went according to the plan. Keith's father drove him to Lancaster and checked him in.

Just as his therapist predicted, Keith called me the first night crying and pleading with me to come get him. He claimed his therapist had put him in "a dump". He promised that if I came and got him, I could take him anywhere else.

For all I knew, the place might have been a dump. I had never seen it. But that had no bearing on the fact that he needed help and had to stay there. I told him I knew the process would be difficult for him but he had to find a way to deal with it.

I hated to have to spend the sixth month of my pregnancy alone, but looked forward to the peace and quiet I would have without him.

Before Keith left, I told him I wanted to hire a contractor to build a closet in the dormer that would soon become the baby's room. He mentioned that he knew a carpenter and would arrange it.

He hired the guy and gave him a couple hundred dollars for materials to get things started. Keith told him I would give him the balance after he completed the job.

The contractor used the money Keith gave him to buy some lumber. Then he brought it to our house and haphazardly dumped it in the first-floor hallway.

On the first day, after working just a few hours, he asked me for money to buy more supplies. As far as I knew, Keith had not agreed to that, but he somehow convinced me to give him fifty dollars. He took the money and did not come back for the rest of the day.

He left without cleaning anything up. Wood scraps and screws remained wherever he had dropped them. The wood he had dumped in the hallway completely obstructed it. I couldn't move any of it because it weighed too much.

His carelessness and lack of consideration really irked me, but I figured I could put up with it for a few days; until he finished the job.

The guy showed up the next morning asking for another fifty dollars. He claimed I had not given him enough money the day before to buy the supplies he needed. He said he could not continue the job without them.

I told him I had to discuss it with Keith first.

He said he would stop back the next morning. If I had fifty dollars for him, he would continue the job.

Keith had not told me how he knew the carpenter, but I quickly figured out he had to be some kind of addict friend. Keith must have made some kind of shady arrangement with the guy and left me with yet another mess to deal with.

Though I wanted to fire the addict/carpenter, I feared retaliation. Aware that my husband would be away the entire month, I worried about what he might do.

The guy showed up the next morning, still complaining he could not finish the job without more money.

I asserted that I had no more money to give him.

He left and never returned.

I hired another carpenter to take the job over. He completed the project in a few days and left the house immaculate.

It took two weeks to straighten all that out. Rehab family week coincided with Keith's third week. I did not have to go but I wanted to show Keith my support.

Seven months pregnant, in the dead of winter of 1985, I drove to Lancaster, Pennsylvania, and checked myself into The Terraces for a week's stay.

Our family group, all parents of addicts except for me, had different workshops each day—some with our addicts, some without.

They called Keith's group, all cocaine addicts, The Coconuts.

We had papers to write and homework assignments to complete every night. The mental strain exhausted me. And because most of the addicts had substituted cigarettes for their drug of choice, I could barely get a clean breath of air for an entire week. I could not wait to get out of there and go home.

Keith still had one more week left to go. He could not wait to come home either.

I planned to pick him up on the morning of his release, and then we would drive to Philadelphia for a romantic weekend.

On the morning of Keith's discharge, I awoke to the aftermath of a snowy blizzard. Judging by the substantial accumulation and sizeable snowdrifts outside the house, I could tell that the storm had raged all night.

The roads in front and on the side of our house were thickly blanketed with unspoiled virgin snow. The snowplow had yet to come.

As much as I hated to disappoint Keith, I did not see how I, seven months pregnant, could drive to Lancaster under those conditions. Though eager to get out of there, I hoped Keith would not want to jeopardize my safety or that of his unborn child.

He called at nine a.m. to ask what time I would be picking him up, unaware of the weather conditions back home.

I explained the problem to him, expecting him to tell me to stay home. Instead, he ranted and raved. He insisted I come get him out of there.

I felt conflicted. I understood what drove his anger. After being sequestered for thirty days, he wanted his freedom. Still, I could not believe his lack of consideration for my welfare and that of his unborn child. Yet a part of me felt sorry for him.

I told him to call back in an hour and I would see if I could arrange it. I hung up the phone and called my father for advice, certain he would have my best interests at heart.

My father did not think the main roads or highways would be nearly as hazardous as the side streets appeared to be. He offered to drive to Lancaster himself and bring Keith home.

I appreciated his offer. At least I had a viable option. But if my father picked him up, we would have to forfeit our weekend together in Philly.

I opened the front door and looked outside. The snow had stopped falling. A few of our neighbors had started shoveling their walks and clearing off their cars.

It had not snowed in Lancaster or Philadelphia and they were not in the path of the storm.

I called my father back to ask how he felt about me driving there alone. He assured me that once I reached the highway, I should not have any problems. He offered to come over and clean off my car. I gratefully accepted.

When Keith called me back, I had good news for him. I would be there by noon.

The Guidance Whisperer

....

Sometimes, perhaps, we are allowed to get lost that we may find the right person to ask directions of. ~Robert Brault

....

So much had transpired in the thirty days we had been apart. We had each experienced major shifts in our outlooks. The Philadelphia trip gave us an opportunity to reconnect in a neutral environment.

The man I met and fell in love with had finally come back to me. I wanted to savor every minute of our weekend together.

There were so many things Keith wanted to share with me.

He apologized over and over for all he had put me through and how much he had hurt me. He said that the thought of doing that to me constantly tortured him.

He talked about all the experiences he had at The Terraces and the friends he had made.

He came clean about his cocaine addiction and told me how it began, explained the calamitous influence it had over him, and described the hellish places his addiction had taken him to.

We shared our hopes and dreams for the baby.

Keith could not wait to be a father. Still certain we were having a girl, he mused over all the things he would do and share with her.

I knew better than to ask about his sobriety. If wishes made it so he would never use again, but he would never make false promises to me about his addiction. His life would be a perpetual uphill climb. Whether or not he could withstand the pressure, no one could say.

I desperately wanted to save my marriage and provide a stable, emotionally healthy, two-parent home for our child. Keith had been given all the tools and resources he needed to stay clean. But the only promise he could ever make to himself and me was to face his addiction one day at a time.

When we returned home, Keith immersed himself in the Narcotics Anonymous Twelve-Step Program. He went to at least one meeting every day. And as recommended, he severed all associations with other addicts not in a twelve-step program. His diabolical brother headed up that list.

I knew he constantly struggled with drug cravings but he still seemed reasonably happy. The impending birth of our baby gave him a goal to focus on. He managed his life one day at a time and I tried my best not to worry.

Keith's addiction had become my addiction. I had lived my life on the edge, scrutinizing his words and actions, wondering when my world would crumble again. I had allowed him to define my happiness and control every aspect of my life.

Living that way did not help him and it destroyed me. He would either sink or swim but I had to get well for the sake of my baby.

My week at The Terraces had taught me a lot. They had given me the tools I needed to deal with the many aspects of Keith's addiction and recovery.

The counselors strongly encouraged the family members to attend Nar-Anon meetings when we got back home. They stressed how valuable that support would be for us.

I never imagined myself participating in a Twelve-Step program. The thought of walking into a room full of strangers made me uncomfortable, but I knew I should give it a chance. I did need the support and friendship it could offer me.

I felt odd walking into my first meeting, but the people were so warm and welcoming, my discomfort quickly subsided.

The meeting began with The Serenity prayer said in unison. Then the chairperson asked if anyone would like to "share".

The first person sharing stated his or her first name and the entire group responded, "Hi (name of the person)," in unison. After the person had spoken, the group as a whole responded, "Thanks for sharing. Keep coming back." No one offered advice, no one judged.

I chose to share next. Following their lead, I stated my first name, my reason for attendance, and then explained my situation. I felt the group's warmth and compassion as they patiently listened to my story.

As I sat there listening to others share, I leafed through the Nar-Anon handbook and silently read the first three steps of the twelve-step program.

1. We admitted we were powerless over the addict—that our lives had become unmanageable.
2. Came to believe that a Power greater than ourselves could restore us to sanity.
3. Made a decision to turn our will and our lives over to the care of God as we understood Him.

I did not believe I had any work to do on the first step. I had already come to terms with my lack of power over Keith's addiction, and understood with every fiber of my being that my life had become unmanageable.

The second and third steps concerned me. I had no belief in a Power greater than myself or any understanding of God. In fact, I did not buy into the God concept at all. It made no sense to me.

As a child, my mother's hypocritical representation of Judaism turned me off to the whole God thing. And six years in Hebrew School learning about a supposedly loving, kind God who could turn into a judgmental, vindictive, and angry one at will, made me reject the concept even more.

I explained my dilemma to the chairwoman.

She pointed out that a Higher Power did not have to be God or something spiritual; it could be anything I wanted it to be.

That eased my mind and helped me better understand the concept.

I went home and gave it some thought. I had no faith in God but had always believed in the power of love. I realized I had always had a Higher Power. It was "Love".

More comfortable and familiar with the Nar-Anon way, I began attending meetings a few times each week. I got to know the regulars and developed a kinship with them.

People go to Nar-Anon family meetings to share their feelings, learn from each other's experiences, and offer each other support. No one is supposed to offer advice.

For that reason, I paid particularly close attention to the words of wisdom offered to me in private one evening by our chairwoman.

"As parents of addicts, we are burdened with our problems for the rest of our lives. We have no choice but to accept our situation. You are still young and you have your whole life ahead of you. You don't have to try so hard. You can walk away from all of this and move on with your life."

Though unprepared to hear those words, the message she conveyed made perfect sense to me. Still, I felt I had to defend my position. Questioning my own words as I spoke them, my answer sounded uncertain.

"I married him to spend our lives together. I promised to love him for good or bad, in sickness and in health. I am trying to keep my promise, to stand by him and make our marriage work."

She responded, "Just keep in mind that you don't have to."

Paper Sunglasses

....

If I am thinking correctly, said Pooh, a new baby is probably undoubtedly the grandest gift that could ever be. ~Winnie the Pooh

....

With my due date right around the corner, I went into nesting mode. I stayed busy organizing everything I could get my hands on.

Besides having been sick and bedridden for the first trimester, my pregnancy had gone smoothly. I had experienced no complications despite the terrible stress I had been under for most of it.

Two weeks and six days before my actual due date, I began leaking amniotic fluid. I went to see my doctor and he sent me to the hospital.

On May 6, 1985, at 5:38 P.M I gave birth by Cesarean section to a five-pound eight-ounce perfectly healthy baby girl. Keith stood by my side during the entire surgery witnessing the joyous birth of our daughter.

We named her Cameryn April and planned to call her Cammy.

After giving birth, I held my baby just long enough to count her fingers and toes and admire her pretty little ears. Then they whisked her away to the nursery and sent me to recovery.

Keith and all four grandparents alternately kept an eye on her in the nursery but I did not get to see her again for almost twenty-four hours. It upset me that the nurses would not bring her to me sooner. I ached to hold her.

Because of my surgery, the doctor required me to stay in the hospital for five days. I had the option of having the baby room-in with me overnight or sending her to the nursery so I could sleep. I wanted to take care of her myself so I chose to keep her with me. I only allowed them to take her down to the nursery when the doctors needed to examine her.

One morning, a nurse came to my room to get Cammy and take her to the nursery. I handed her over without a second thought as I had done every time they asked me to.

After the nurse had taken the baby and left the room, my mother, who was visiting with me at the time, looked at me strangely. She asked if I had ever seen that nurse before. She said she had noticed that the nurse had no badge on.

It annoyed me that my mother had not mentioned anything about the badge before the nurse left with the baby. I did not recognize her, but that did not concern me. They always sent someone different up from the nursery.

My mother had a way of saying things without actually saying them but I always knew what she meant. This time, she was insinuating that someone might have just stolen my baby. I went into panic mode.

If that had been my grandchild, I would have gotten up and followed the lady who took the baby; not passively sat there frightening my daughter and watching her worry herself sick.

I called down to the nursery to ask if my baby had gotten there safely. The lady told me that Cammy had not gotten there yet, but that the nursery staff had sent someone up to my room to get her.

She asked me to hold on for a minute so she could check it out and then came back on the phone to tell me that Cammy had just arrived.

I could not have been more relieved. After such a fright, it took a while for me to calm down. It angered me that my mother had put me through such unnecessary trauma.

Cammy developed infant jaundice, a common condition, on her fourth day.

Many babies develop infant jaundice after they have already gone home. In mild cases, it disappears on its own within two or three weeks. Since Cammy's jaundice developed during our hospital stay, they had to treat it before releasing her.

The method of treatment for infant jaundice is phototherapy. The baby is placed on her back under special lights for between twenty-four to forty-eight hours wearing only a diaper and protective eye patches.

Cammy was a breastfed baby, so I had to go down to the nursery every three hours to feed her. She looked so cute the first time I saw her with her paper "sunglasses" on.

When I came down three hours later, I found her lying on her back staring straight up at the light with no eye protection. None of the nurses had noticed she had pulled it off.

I started screaming, "My baby's gonna be blind, my baby's gonna be blind! Who's supposed to be watching my baby?"

The nurse on duty hurried over, put the patches back over Cammy's eyes, and told me to calm down. She said I was upsetting all the other babies.

She claimed that the patch had just come off and the limited exposure would not damage the baby's eyes.

I saw no reason why I should calm down. I had already witnessed her gross negligence and had no faith in her professional opinion.

Not wanting to stress out my baby or upset the entire nursery, I forced myself to get a grip. The nurse looked down her nose at me, then picked up Cammy and put her in my arms so I could feed her.

When I returned to my room in the middle of the night, I called my pediatrician and left an urgent message. He called me right back, half-asleep, to tell me not to worry. He assured me that he would examine her eyes later that morning.

Thankfully, Cammy's eyes were undamaged.

To avoid dealing with more hormonal lunacy from this neurotic first-time mother, the nurses did not let that happen again—at least not to my baby.

Because of her condition, Cammy had to remain in the hospital two days longer than I did. The doctor offered me the choice of staying there with her or going home. I refused to leave the hospital without my baby.

I proudly celebrated my first Mother's Day on Sunday, May 12, 1985, in the hospital. Keith came to visit in the late morning, my parents and in-laws came in the afternoon.

Around eight o'clock that evening, long after my visitors had gone home, my private telephone rang. I picked up the receiver and heard my mother-in-law's voice on the other end. Her caustic tone scared me.

Clearly intoxicated, she started off by telling me what a good-for-nothing husband I had. She contended that while I lay in the hospital with his baby, Keith was home getting loaded.

She claimed that Keith had been too messed up to buy his own Mother's Day gift for me and had asked her to buy it for him.

Before abruptly ending the call, she said that Keith had instructed her to put my gift in a brown paper bag and leave it in the back of my closet. She said it angered her that he planned to take all the credit.

Dumbstruck by her vengeful allegations, I only uttered two words the entire time; "Okay" and "Bye".

Having been on the receiving end of her nasty, drunken rampage before, I doubted her malicious allegations.

I got out of bed to investigate. Sure enough, I found the brown paper bag with a bottle of my mother-in-law's favorite perfume exactly where she claimed she had left it. Keith would have never picked that gift out for me. I knew she had told me the truth.

Recovering from surgery and exhausted from the demands of a

new baby, I did not have the energy to get into it with Keith. What was the point anyway? I had heard enough lies, excuses, and empty promises.

And just like that, the joy of my very first Mother's Day along with all my hopes and dreams for our family were shattered. I could no longer kid myself. My husband had an ungovernable, incurable disease that he would never recover from and I could do nothing about it.

With an infant to take care of, I did not have the luxury of a prolonged pity-party. I had allowed my own suffering for many years, but I refused to let anyone or anything hurt Cammy.

Cammy's jaundice resolved itself and we were scheduled to go home the next day. Keith had brought the infant car seat up to my room before he left earlier in the day so we were ready to go.

He promised to call me first thing in the morning to find out what time to pick us up. After seven days in the hospital, I could not wait to bring Cammy home.

The nurse advised me early the next morning that our discharge time was eleven a.m. Anticipating Keith's call, I quickly showered and dressed in regular clothes for the first time in a week.

At ten a.m., still no word from Keith, I fed the baby, changed her diaper, and dressed her in her new going-home outfit.

Getting impatient, I called Keith at home and then at work, but I could not find him anywhere. I figured he might be on his way to the hospital.

Eleven o'clock came and went with no word from Keith. He knew how badly I wanted to go home. I could not imagine how long he expected me to wait. Frustrated by his lack of consideration, I alternated between pacing the floor and sitting in the chair nervously tapping my foot.

When twelve o'clock rolled around and I still had not heard from him, I decided to make other arrangements. I called my father, told him what had happened, and asked him to pick us up. He said he would leave right away and be there in twenty minutes.

Ten minutes after I talked to my father, Keith called. He asked what time he should pick us up.

I responded icily with two words, "Don't bother."

He asked me why.

I told him my father would be taking us home.

His tone completely changed. He started bullying me; declaring that *he* was the father and no one else was going to take *his* baby home. He told me he would be there shortly and ordered me to wait for him.

Exhausted from everything I had been through, I did not care who picked us up. I just wanted to go home.

My father arrived first. I told him that Keith had called and he wanted to take us home. He understood and said he'd be happy to wait there with me. I felt comforted having him there.

When Keith arrived, my father happily assisted with escorting Cammy and me out of the hospital, then into the car.

And then finally, with the baby securely fastened in her infant car seat, we headed home.

Escaping the Danger Zone

One of the hardest things you will ever have to do, my dear, is grieve the loss of a person who is still alive. ~Jeanette Walls, The Glass Castle

Keith had dreamed Cammy to life down to the very last detail. She even looked like him.

If the pride and adoration he had for his daughter could not keep him straight then nothing could. But I had no grand delusions. I knew he could bottom out at any time.

With all the demands of having a new baby to care for, I had no time to concern myself with Keith's sobriety.

Cammy slept a great deal the first four weeks of her life. I found it difficult to keep her awake long enough during feedings to sustain her for more than two hours at a time.

I got no sleep and barely got to eat. Whenever she smelled food, she would wake up from a sound sleep crying.

I wish I could say she helped me lose weight but that did not happen. I compensated by wolfing down whatever I could eat before she caught me.

Cammy's grandparents rejoiced over her birth. She was the

first grandchild on both sides of the family, so they had all gone grandparent crazy.

Since I had not gotten clearance from my doctor to walk steps or drive when it was time for Cammy's two-week pediatric check-up, Keith's mother volunteered to take her.

Capitalizing on the first opportunity to spoil her granddaughter, she insisted on driving her to the doctor's office in her Rolls Royce. From the very beginning, Grandma would see to it that her only grandchild had nothing but the best.

My parents were overcome with joy over their new grandbaby. In their immodest opinion, a more special child had never been born.

Keith seemed to keep his drug habit in check for the first month. We played the "don't ask don't tell" game. But before long, he began spiraling out of control again.

First, he began showing signs of paranoia. After coming home from work, he would walk from window to window closing each blind. The bay window in the living room did not have a covering, so he used thumbtacks to hang a sheet in front of it. I also kept noticing him peeking outside.

Sometimes he would carry a dining room chair to the front of the house and jam the back of it under the doorknob.

Though unsure what would finally push me out the door, I suspected it would not take long.

Sadly, I still loved my husband very much. Call me crazy, but I could not bear the thought of being without him. I thought I needed him in my life to be happy. We were both sick but in different ways.

One evening, Keith offered to go out and pick up steamed crabs for dinner. We rarely ate them so I looked forward to it.

He claimed he did not have enough cash in his wallet to buy them (and he had no credit cards), so he hoped that his "friend" would cash a check.

His "friend" owned a Chinese restaurant not far from our house. According to Keith, the guy had cashed checks for him before so he did not think there would be a problem.

Cliffedge Road

The carryout place where he planned to get the crabs could not have been more than a mile from the Chinese restaurant. He promised he would be right back.

In the meantime, I covered the dining room table with newspaper, laid out the knives and mallets, and filled a pitcher of water. I fed the baby hoping she would sleep while we ate. Then I waited.

Nearly two hours passed before Keith returned home. He walked into the den where I was sitting, the smell of Old Bay seasoning emanating from the damp brown paper bag clenched in his hand. Keith had glassy eyes and was stumbling.

I took one look at him and cried, "You are unbelievable!"

He looked confused. He did not seem to understand why I might be angry at him.

"I brought you the crabs?"

I picked up the baby and marched upstairs. Then grabbing the first suitcase I could find, hurriedly threw in some clothing and necessities for Cammy and me.

Keith had barely figured out what had happened before I dashed out the door with Cammy in my arms and drove away. I did not have a destination in mind—just the compulsion to run.

After driving aimlessly for more than twenty minutes, I spotted a hotel off the side of the highway. The adrenaline rush had worn off and I felt weary. I needed a quiet place to gather my thoughts. I exited the highway, drove into the hotel parking lot, and booked a room for the night.

I checked out of the hotel at around six a.m. the next morning and then headed home, expecting Keith to have already left for work. I hoped to avoid a confrontation.

As I neared the house, I saw his white pickup truck parked outside. He typically would have been gone by then.

I parked my car around the corner and waited for him to leave. After forty-five minutes of waiting, his pickup truck remained in front of the house. He did not appear to be going anywhere and

I could not sit in the car all day with the baby, so I pulled my car around to the front of the house and parked.

No sooner did I step out of my car when my next-door neighbor approached me. She asked me if everything was all right. I asked why she wanted to know. She explained that the police had come to my house at nine o'clock the previous night. I told her I had spent the night away from home and knew nothing about it.

It did not surprise me that the police had showed up, though I wondered what precipitated the visit the night before. They had come to our house before but Keith had instructed me to never answer the door.

Love or no love, I would have to get the baby and myself out of that house as soon as possible.

I could not bear to think about leaving Shane and Honeybell behind, but from that point on, I knew I would have to make difficult choices. I hoped to eventually find a place for all of us to live. With no job, no money, and no potential source of income, that would not happen anytime soon.

I could not kick Keith out of the house because he never added my name to the title. Now I understood why.

Keith heard me come in the house and met me at the door, angrily hurling verbal threats at me. Refusing to take his crap any longer, I got right up in his face and gave it all back to him.

The upheaval upset the baby and she started to cry. I told him I had nothing more to say, and then headed upstairs to nurse Cammy and rock her to sleep. Keith followed right behind.

Once the baby had quieted down, I laid her in the crib and then went to finish up with Keith who had been waiting for me in the bedroom.

I told him I could no longer tolerate his addiction and had nothing more to give; that Cammy and I would be moving out as soon as I found somewhere for us to live.

He cried and pleaded with me to give him another chance but I told him he had used up all his chances. He begged me not to leave. I told him it was too late for that. I had already made my decision.

Then his tone changed and he started bullying me. He lectured, "You can't leave. You have no money, no job, and nowhere to live. You'll never survive without me. If you leave again, don't ever expect to come back!"

When I refused to argue back, his anger escalated. In desperation, he walked into Cammy's room and lifted her out of her crib. Holding her tight against his chest, he threatened, "Fine, you can leave but the baby stays with me!"

The Keith I had known before would never have harmed her. But his behavior, now unstable and unpredictable, worried me.

Fearful he might do something desperate but trying to appear calm, I asked him to please hand me the baby. He refused. I asked him again and he refused again. I had no more time to waste on negotiations.

I lunged for the phone and dialed 911. Keith tried to grab it out of my hand but I held on tight. As fast as possible, I explained the urgency of the problem. The dispatcher said she would send an officer to the house right away.

I looked up at Keith's face and watched his demeanor change again. He stood there staring at me in disbelief as if the reality of the situation had suddenly slapped him across the face.

A shroud of sadness overcame him. The forlorn look in his eyes said it all. He knew he had just lost everything.

Keith would not let Cammy go until the sudden sound of the police officer rapping on the front door startled him. Acknowledging in his way that he knew his time had run out, he kissed Cammy on her head and gently handed her back to me.

I ran down the steps with Cammy in my arms and answered the door.

I explained everything to the officer and told him I believed, at least for the time being, that things were under control. I asked him to write up a police report anyway. I wanted a record of the incident in case something happened later on.

Once everything had settled down, Keith left the house and went to work, or wherever he went during the day.

I had little time to waste in figuring out my next move. I grabbed the yellow pages, looked up safe houses and shelters, and then made some calls.

I knew my parents would welcome us with open arms, but after living on my own for eight years, the last thing I wanted to do was run back to Mom and Dad; back to the chaotic, drama-infused environment that had destroyed my childhood. I would be going from the fire into the frying pan.

On the other hand, I had no doubt that their home would be physically safe for Cammy and that she would be showered with love and attention there.

There were no easy answers. I had taken an inadvisable gamble on Keith's sobriety. The time had come to face the consequences of that decision.

My best interests no longer mattered. Whatever choices I made from that moment on had to be in the best interests of my daughter.

Keith came home later that afternoon acting as if nothing had happened. In an effort to avoid another confrontation, I kept my distance from him. When he went downstairs, I went upstairs and vice versa. He eventually came upstairs, got into bed, and went to sleep for the night. I breathed a sigh of relief.

Free to roam the house as I pleased with the baby sleeping upstairs in her crib, I tiptoed barefooted downstairs and headed for the kitchen to get a drink of water.

After taking two steps into the kitchen, I gasped and froze dead in my tracks. The fractured base of a drinking glass with a four-inch jagged spike pointing straight up sat erect in the middle of the kitchen floor. Shattered glass fragments were scattered in every direction. One more step and I probably would have severed an artery.

Cliffedge Road

Within the span of two days, my life with Keith had changed from unstable to perilous. My home had become a danger zone. I had just barely avoided stepping on a land mine. I could not imagine what other dangers or booby traps lurked ahead.

I told myself I only had to hang in there until tomorrow, just until after Keith left for work. Then I would pack up and leave forever.

At around one o'clock in the morning, I awoke to the sound of the baby crying. Keith was no longer sleeping next to me in bed.

I thought he might be in Cammy's room and definitely did not want him spending any time alone with her, so I got up to investigate.

When I couldn't find him in the nursery, I figured he had gone downstairs. I didn't know where he had gone or why. I only knew he had to be up to no good.

Heading down the steps to look for him, I noticed the front door was wide open. I hurried down the rest of the steps and looked outside. Keith and his car were gone.

I locked the door and laid in wait for him on the living room sofa.

Over an hour later, he knocked on the door. Totally surprised to find the door locked and me waiting there, he blurted out some bogus story about going to 7-Eleven to get cigarettes. He claimed he had left the door open because he did not have a key.

Out of everything Keith had ever put me through, that act of negligence scared me the most. After what I had survived a few years before, he knew how imperative the security of the house was for me, especially while I slept. How dare he leave the baby and me vulnerable and defenseless that way.

The time had come. I could not compromise our safety one minute longer.

I called my parents and woke them up. I told them the baby and I were all right but that Keith had relapsed again. I asked if I could come over and talk. They told me they would be up and waiting for me.

With that, Cammy and I were out the door.

We sat down in their living room as I recounted the unstable conditions we had endured over the past month. We all decided it would be best for Cammy and me to leave Keith right away and move in with them.

I stayed at their house until seven in the morning, the time Keith usually left for work. Then, leaving Cammy safe with my parents, I went home to pack up whatever I could fit in my car.

I tearfully kissed and hugged my babies Shane and Honeybell and told them I loved them. Keith loved the dogs too and I knew he would manage to take care of them—for a little while at least. I hoped to come back and rescue them as soon as I could get on my feet.

I walked out the door. Then halfway down the path, I turned around and looked back at the house. With tears streaming down my face, I said a final goodbye to my life and all my shattered dreams at Cliffedge Road.

THREE STIPULATIONS

....

The saddest thing about betrayal is that it never comes from your enemies. ~Unknown

....

Later that morning, I called Keith's parents to ask if I could come over for a visit. They had been dangling from the same last thread of hope as I had. I dreaded the thought of having to tell them the bad news.

Understandably, they took it very hard. Though acknowledging the same hopelessness as I had felt with their son, they still struggled with where to place their loyalties. I could not blame them. For a long time, I had struggled with the same thing.

So distraught after hearing the news, they decided then and there to leave town the next day for an indefinite Florida stay.

I slept at my parents' house that night. The next day, my father suggested we go back to the Cliffedge Road house to get Cammy's crib and anything else I did not want destroyed. Though I never wanted to enter that house again, I agreed with my father. We had to move fast.

I tried using my key to unlock the front door and it would not work at first. It took some finagling but I finally managed to get the door open. Once inside the house, we could see that Keith had jammed a toothpick in the lock. He had also left the dining room chair by the door, apparently for reinforcement.

First, we dismantled the crib. Then we carried it outside along with the matching chest of drawers and loaded the items in the car.

Next, we emptied the china cabinet. Together, we carefully wrapped my china, silver, and crystal wedding gifts in the newspaper and boxes that my father had wisely brought along. I took anything I thought I would need and everything of value. I only waffled on one thing; Keith's baseball card collection.

Keith had saved every baseball card he had ever gotten for the last twenty-five or more years. He had a box full of them in the basement; many were valuable. I had no entitlement to them but I also had no money. I could have possibly liquidated them for some cash. But even believing he would somehow destroy them or sell them to buy drugs, I just did not have the heart to take them. I pitied him. He had so very little left.

Cammy was twelve weeks old when we left Keith and moved out of the Cliffedge Road house. I had never intended to raise her as a single parent but sometimes life throws you curveballs. Nobody knew that better than I did.

With limited hindsight at my young age, I could draw only one conclusion; my life would always be a struggle. Trauma and tragedy would follow me wherever I went.

I could not make sense of my past but I never played victim or blamed anyone. I took full responsibility for my problems and the decisions I had made that contributed to them.

Though I despised Keith's illness and all the insanity that came with it, I never stopped loving him—the man I met and fell in love with. Although rare, there were spurts of time when that lovable person shined through. Unfortunately, those times were overshadowed by his impossible behavior.

Sometimes we fall in love with an illusion of a person that was never really there. This was different. The real Keith *was* there. I met him. I knew him. He loved me as much, if not more than I loved him.

Our relationship was destined to be—just not forever.

I hoped to keep things amicable between us; I wanted Cammy to know her father. But that became difficult.

Keith could not bear the thought of losing me and desperately tried to keep me in his life any way he could. He used what little control he had left over me to prolong the inevitable. I never planned to make things hard on him, but he eventually forced my hand and left me no choice.

He retained his family's lawyer immediately. I hesitated to get an attorney because I could not afford the exorbitant fees and did not want to burden my parents with the expense.

I tried to be as flexible as possible when it came to Keith's visitations with Cammy. I set three non-negotiable stipulations:

1. He could not be high
2. The visits had to be on my turf
3. I had to supervise all his interactions with her.

Knowing he had to cooperate in order to see his daughter, he exhibited only his best behavior—at first. Each week for the first month of our separation, he voluntarily brought me a hundred dollars.

I appreciated his effort, but I could not live and take care of a baby on four hundred dollars a month. I asked him to commit to pay at least two hundred dollars a week and continue paying our health insurance coverage.

The more I tried to pin him down to an agreement, the less he cooperated. Before long, his compliance waned. He became more belligerent with each passing day.

On one of his visits, I asked him to bring whatever mail he had for me the next time he came over. I had sent out change of address notifications but thought that some things might have crossed in the mail.

Keith claimed I had not received anything important—only junk mail. His evasiveness seemed suspicious. I had not received two particular statements and figured he probably had them. I still had a key to his house so I could easily poke around and look for them when he wasn't there.

I went to the house the next day during his regular work hours. When I tried to open the front door with my key, the lock would not budge. So, I walked around to the backyard and tried my key in the kitchen door lock. Tada! The door opened.

I did not have to look very far. All his opened mail, including my department store credit card bill and my bank statement, laid spread out on the dining room table.

I found a bill from a lock and key service dated two days prior. That explained why I could not open the front door with my key.

Things had begun to escalate.

Keith's once relaxed visits turned into angry exchanges between him and my parents.

I asked them not to interfere but they had no self-control. My parents and I quarreled every time he left.

Keith threatened that if my parents ordered him one more time not to kiss the baby on her mouth or to be careful not to bump her head, he would take her away from me.

He demanded I allow him overnight visits with Cammy at his house every other weekend. He knew I would never agree to that. He just wanted to aggravate me.

I wanted no more interaction with him, verbal or otherwise, until I retained an attorney. And I definitely did not want him anywhere near Cammy.

Angry that he could not see Cammy, he began persistently calling my parents' house, refusing to speak to anyone but me. My parents never put his calls through. Each time he called, they told him to have his attorney contact me. At least when it came to Cammy, they were fierce protectors.

In desperation, he finally called and told my father that if he couldn't speak to me directly he would break into the house, take the baby, and go someplace where we would never find them.

Keith had begun to frighten me. I couldn't handle him myself.

My parents graciously offered to pay my legal expenses. I hated to use their savings but Keith had my back to the wall.

I arranged to meet with the attorney that represented my best friend Carolyn's family. From that day forward, all communication went through our lawyers.

Still, I worried myself sick. I feared a judge might grant Keith unsupervised visits or shared custody. I had witnessed Keith con and manipulate judges before in court. My fears were not irrational. He was a pro.

The Final Rescue

··········

To love an addict is to run out of tears. ~Sandy Swenson

··········

I cried myself to sleep every night for the first two months of our separation. I could barely stand the emptiness I felt inside. Had it not been for Cammy, I do not know how I could have pushed forward. She lit and brightened my otherwise gloomy outlook.

I knew I needed help but did not know what for. I could not afford a therapist so I went to the library and checked out every self-help book that spoke to me.

One day, I stumbled upon a book by Robin Norwood entitled *Women Who Love Too Much*. The synopsis on the back seemed as if she had written it about me. I checked the book out and read it from cover to cover.

That heaven-sent book fundamentally changed my life. For the first time ever, I saw my self-destructive codependent patterns and understood how my choices impacted the outcomes of my life. That awareness shook me out of the fog I had been in for so many years. It empowered me to take charge of my life and redirect the course of it in an emotionally healthy way.

I needed a job but did not qualify to earn more than minimum wage. That kind of income would never get me and Cammy out of my parents' house. I did not want to live under their supervision one day longer than I had to.

I learned of a one-year Optical Assistant certification program being offered by a local community college. The subject matter interested me. I knew I would never get rich with that qualification, but I could find a decent job in the eye-care field once I graduated.

My parents generously offered to pay for my schooling. My semi-retired father selflessly volunteered to give up his part-time job in order to stay home with Cammy while I attended classes.

They had rescued us and given us a place to live. They showered Cammy with an abundance of love, affection, and attention. They were sacrificing everything for us. I felt immensely grateful for the many ways they were helping to protect Cammy and get me back on my feet.

I felt indebted to them for the rest of my life. Yet I thought I would lose my mind living with them.

The lunacy of their behavior made it impossible to live peacefully. And while they had done everything, supposedly with the intention of getting me back on my feet, I knew they would resent me taking Cammy away from them. I felt terribly guilty about my conflicted feelings.

No matter. I would allow nothing or no one to stop me from taking my life back.

Keith continued playing his games, trying to keep me in a holding pattern.

In an attempt to avoid expensive litigation, my attorney tried to negotiate an out of court settlement with his attorney.

Antagonizing me in a way only Keith could, he agreed to give me everything I asked for; with just one provision. I had to sign a legal document agreeing to allow him one unsupervised overnight visit each week with Cammy, after her first birthday.

He knew I would never agree to that. He just used it as a stall tactic and to justify his refusal of everything else I asked for.

Keith submitted himself to an outpatient methadone program.

I presumed he did that on the advice of his attorney. The highly monitored treatment plan kept him out of danger for a while, but unfortunately, did not stabilize his erratic behavior.

On the morning of October 20th, Keith called my parents' house to talk to me. I had already left for school so he asked them to please have me call him back.

When I got home, I called him back but got a busy signal. I tried several more times throughout the afternoon and evening but kept getting a busy signal. I figured he had taken his phone off the hook.

I heard nothing from him until four days later when he called to ask if he could see the baby.

I asked if he had pulled himself together.

He scoffed, "Together as I can be," then began screaming irrationally into the phone, blaming me for causing his nervous breakdown.

I hung right up on him. He did not call back.

Two days after that, Keith's mother called from Florida to speak with me. My mother talked to her because I was still sleeping.

She apprised my mother, albeit unclearly, of an emergency situation that had arisen with Keith. All my mother could relay to me was that it had something to do with him going through a window and not injuring himself.

She told my mother that she had booked a flight and would arrive in Baltimore later that day.

I awoke shortly after my mother hung up with her and then called right back. Keith's father answered the phone. He explained that Keith had been spiraling downhill for the last week or so and that they truly believed he had lost his mind—that it might be necessary to have him institutionalized.

He advised that Cammy and I stay away from him in the meantime because they had no idea what he might do.

When I hung up the phone with him, I called Keith. Surprisingly, he picked up the telephone. He tried to speak but was so despondent he could only blubber. His state of mind alarmed me. I feared he might be suicidal.

I assured Keith that everything would be alright. I stressed how much Cammy needed her Daddy.

I told him to get dressed; I would be over soon to take him to a doctor.

I had previously explained Keith's situation to a doctor friend of mine who specialized in holistic medicine. He thought he might be able to help.

As we drove to the doctor's office, his moods shifted wildly. My father-in-law had not exaggerated his condition. Keith was definitely in a state of psychosis.

The pen quivered spastically between his fingers as he struggled to fill in the patient profile sheet in the waiting room. He could not recall basic information. He listed me as head of household and asked me for my last name.

My friend examined him and suggested a treatment plan. In order to achieve results, he would have to commit to the regimen. He agreed to follow through, but I knew he would not. It did not matter either way. I had no attachment to the outcome.

We left the office and I had not driven a block before Keith started screaming at me. He demanded I stop the car. Without saying a word, he opened the car door and got out, then slammed the door closed and started walking away.

Relieved to be rid of him, I drove away and left him rambling down the road.

Keith's mother called later in the day to let me know she had arrived. I asked if she had talked to Keith yet, wondering if he had made it home.

She haughtily declared that she would not be seeing or speaking to Keith. She did not even want him knowing she had come to Baltimore because she feared "he might try to kill her."

I found it disturbing how quickly she redirected the focus onto herself.

I asked her how she planned to help him. She said that she had not come to help Keith, only to have him committed or locked up.

I didn't care either way. How she chose to deal or not deal with her son did not matter to me. I had officially washed my hands of the whole mess.

She told me she would be over the next day to see Cammy.

Cammy had only been three months old the last time her Grandma had seen her. Now an adorable six months old, she had become much more animated. My mother-in-law could not get over her.

While visiting, she broke the news that she and Keith's father would never be coming back to Baltimore to live; that my father-in-law would be selling the produce business and retiring. She said that they could no longer bear to stay and face the painful memories.

That must have been an agonizing decision for my father-in-law to make. His entire life revolved around the business he had successfully cultivated from the ground up.

Keith's father had clung to the hope that Keith would someday take over the business when he retired. Now, all hope was lost.

I could certainly understand his exasperation and need to run away. Keith seemed to have that effect on those who loved him.

My mother-in-law visited with us for a few hours and then advised me she would call the next day if she remained in town.

She never called. She must have left town that same night

Over the following week, Keith called me three or more times a day. He even showed up at my door one day. I pretended not to be home to avoid having to deal with him.

Lonely and desperate for someone to talk to, he kept calling to ask if he could see the baby. Each time he asked, I reminded him that he had to see a psychiatrist first because Cammy needed a well daddy. The next day, he would call to tell me he was better.

Sometimes he would call and make up nonsense to keep me on the phone. I tried to be patient but by the end of the week, he had gotten on my last nerve. I asked him to please stop calling; I did not have time to listen to his triviality.

In retaliation, he called me at six-forty-five the next morning just to declare that he would not give me anything I asked for.

I'd had enough of him running me around in circles and playing games. If he wanted to act tough then I would too. I mailed a letter to his attorney stating that Keith could not visit the baby until a professional therapist or psychiatrist advised me of his mental competency.

When Keith learned of the ultimatum I had imposed on him, he punished me by cutting off my child support checks. Then he convinced his parents that I only wanted their money and to destroy their lives and they turned on me too.

After two weeks without any money, I called Keith in desperation. I knew I would have to make a deal with the devil, but I had no choice. He might have been out of his mind in many ways but not when it came to aggravating me.

He told me that his father had sent me a child support check but said he had not opened the envelope yet. I asked him to open it so he could tell me the amount. He refused.

Then he claimed he would like to start paying me one hundred fifty dollars each week, but would be deducting his medical and psychological expenses for the depression I had caused from every payment.

I skipped right over the bullshit and asked him when I would be receiving the check his father sent me. He finally confessed that he had no check for me, but assured me that he would have money for me the next day. I did not hold my breath.

On Friday evening of that week, while thumbing through a local magazine, I saw a realtor ad for Keith's house. It had the word SOLD printed over it. He had never mentioned selling the house, not that he had to, but some of my possessions were still being held hostage there.

Unable to reach him that night, I called the next morning to ask when I could pick up my possessions. He stipulated that I could have my things if he could see Cammy. I reiterated the conditions of visitation. He refused to give me my things then hung up on me.

He knew the terms for visitation but kept trying to get even with me.

On November eighteenth, my attorney sent a letter to Keith's attorney asking for the return of my belongings and explaining my desperate financial circumstances. He never received a response.

In hopes that Keith would step up to the plate financially, I had not yet applied for Social Service benefits. But Keith played too many games. I badly needed financial assistance and could obviously not count on him for child support.

I contacted the Department of Social Services to set up an appointment with a caseworker. I brought all the required documents and went through the entire application process.

The system denied my eligibility for benefits because the value of my car was higher than the allowable assets. They were only willing to give me WIC.

I only had one asset to my name; my Grand Prix. If I had known how the system worked, I would have transferred ownership of the car to my father.

So, before beginning the appeal process, I did exactly that. After several weeks of waiting, they denied me again. That seemed very unfair. Millions of people receive government assistance, many fraudulently. I genuinely needed the benefits and could not get it.

My attorney had worked on my separation and custody case for three months and gotten nowhere. He tried his best to negotiate an out of court settlement, hoping to save my parents money, but Keith had used my passivity to his benefit. Fed up with the cat and mouse game Keith kept playing with me, I decided to terminate my attorney's legal services and hire someone else to represent me.

The expense of hiring a better attorney might have been worth it if I stood to gain anything financially, but I did not. I only asked

Keith to pay his child-support, continue our healthcare coverage, and show up sober for his visitations.

As long as Keith knew he could exert financial control over me, nothing about this process would be easy.

Sweet Revenge

....

I don't like to call it revenge. Returning the favor sounds much nicer. ~Unknown

....

After all I had been through with Keith, the thought of dating sickened me. One would imagine I would find the prospect of dating "normal" guys refreshing. But truthfully, after living with drama for so many years, I worried they would all bore me. Besides, what young guy would want to date a woman still nursing her baby?

But honestly, leaving all insecurities aside, I really did welcome the attention. It helped to fill the emptiness for a little while.

Determined to get my post-pregnant body back into dating shape, I joined a health club. I circuit trained three nights a week. In no time, the baby weight disappeared and I proudly wore a bikini.

I found the optical program at school very interesting and looked forward to attending my classes each day. My grades reflected the enthusiasm I had for the program. I made the Dean's list both semesters. I also made some very nice friends. But best of all, going to school every day redirected the focus of my largely dysfunctional life.

As an adult child living back in my parents' home, desperate for serenity and harmony in the midst of crazy-making behavior, I had come full circle.

I had no personal space to call my own and my parents knew no boundaries.

Whenever Cammy woke up crying, my father would open the door to the bedroom I shared with her, any time of the day or night, and tell me to pick her up.

I did not take that well. I had never said the "F" word to my father. Now furious at his blatant lack of respect for my privacy, I was yelling at him to fuck himself, get out of my fucking room, and screaming whatever other expletives happened to fly out of my mouth at that moment.

I desperately needed to get out of that house but I had to finish school before I could make that happen. With steadfast determination to give Cammy a happy life, I kept my eye on the future and persevered.

In December, my pricey new attorney jumped right on the case and issued a five-page *Complaint for custody and limited divorce* to the circuit court. Among other requests, she asked for the court to sign an Injunction preventing Keith from transferring, disposing of, or selling any of my personal property.

In her cover letter to Keith's attorney, she wrote:

> *I am sure that your client does not need any more legal entanglements at the present time and would ask that you kindly convey to him the importance of returning these items to my client immediately.*

She drafted the letter on December fourth. That left me only nine days to get my belongings out of the Cliffedge Road house before it went to settlement.

Upon receipt of the letter, Keith's attorney advised him to arrange a time with me to claim my belongings. I only wanted the property I had acquired before marriage. The court could decide the rest.

In compliance, Keith named a specific morning that week. He said he would not be home but promised to leave the front door unlocked.

On the arranged morning, I met the mover I'd hired to help me in front of the Cliffedge Road house, and then we walked up to the front door ready to get started. I tried to open the door but could not. Keith had locked me out.

We walked around to the back door, thinking maybe Keith had left that door unlocked, but he had not.

The mover, a nice young guy, looked at me and asked, "Do you want me to go in through the window? I do it all the time."

Fed up with Keith and his games, I said, "Do it!"

The guy walked around to the side of the house and jimmied the living room window open. Then he climbed in, unlocked the front door, and let me in.

"What am I taking?" he asked me.

Adrenaline coursing through my body, my mind bent on revenge, I made an erratic decision. "That bastard is going to pay for lying to me. I'm taking everything!"

Under my direction, the mover carried out my personal belongings and all our new furniture. I took anything and everything of value. I even took the sheets, blanket and comforter right off our bed, and the alarm clock we had shared.

I knew if I did not take what I wanted right then and there, I would never see any of it again. Keith would eventually sell or destroy it all.

I did not consider where all the furniture would go. My parents' small house already busted at the seams with us living there.

My father saw my car pull up to his house with the moving van behind it and came outside to help us. He had rearranged some things in the house to make space for the furniture he expected me to bring home. I met him in the carport with a sheepish look on my face.

The mover got out of his truck and asked, "Where do you want everything?" I turned away from my father and towards the guy, then discreetly raised my index finger while mouthing the words "Wait a minute." He nodded back at me in acknowledgement.

I looked back at my father. "Dad, I've done something crazy." Then I explained the course of events.

It upset him that I had made such a rash decision. Besides the fact that he had nowhere to put all the furniture, he worried about what Keith would say and do when he discovered I had cleaned him out. Coming down from my adrenaline "high", I began to second guess myself.

I did not want to hold the mover up so I told him to unload everything into the carport. My father and I would have to work on a solution after he left.

The driver emptied out the truck then pulled away, leaving us both standing dumbfounded in front of the jam-packed carport.

Not even an hour had passed before Keith called my parents' house to threaten me. He had just come home, found the furniture missing, and was steaming mad.

He demanded that his furniture be returned immediately or he would have me arrested for breaking, entering, and theft. He said he was coming over, as if I should be frightened. Then he hung up on me.

Though I had no way to hide the stolen evidence, I did not worry about Keith reporting me to the police. With all his parole violations and outstanding warrants, they would have immediately arrested him. Still, the whole thing made me nervous. I did not want to deal with Keith's wrath even though I knew he had no power over me.

Within thirty minutes, Keith came strolling on foot down the street toward my parents' house. Heaven knows what had happened to his car. My father and I stood guard over the evidence in the carport.

He swaggered up the driveway, dressed well with his head held high, affecting an air of dignity.

Though he tried to appear big and important, the wind could have blown him over. He looked gaunt and emaciated.

Calmer than I expected and very polite, he spoke authoritatively in a tone meant to intimidate me.

He fired off his usual threats but I did not react. He tried bargaining with me but got nowhere. I told him to leave or I would call the police on him. He backed down but with one last threat—I would be hearing from his lawyer.

That said, he walked back up the street, heading home I suppose.

The Cliffedge Road house never sold. I don't know what happened.

Keith reported the robbery without implicating me, filed a claim with his homeowner's insurance company, and ended up receiving a sizable cash settlement. In the end, he made out better than I did.

As for all the furniture, my father rearranged the house again and managed to fit it all in.

The Plastic Fruit Stand

....

Sometimes when I need a miracle, I look into my daughter's eyes and realize I've already created one. ~Unknown

....

Keith had done everything he could think of to avoid going to court. He feared losing the control he thought he had over me because losing that control meant losing me and Cammy. The poor guy was so sick, so desperate.

On January 6, 1986, in response to the complaint filed by my attorney, The Circuit Court issued a writ of summons to be served in person to Keith within sixty days. Once the server placed the document in Keith's hand, he had thirty days to sign and return it. If he failed to comply, he would lose the case by default.

The Sheriff's office made several unsuccessful attempts to serve Keith. He knew exactly how to spot and dodge the servers. They recommended I hire a private detective to do it.

On January tenth, I scheduled a time for Keith to come over and visit Cammy. I told the private detective that Keith would be walking over, so he waited on the sidewalk up the street, posed as a neighbor. As Keith approached, the detective created a distraction and then put the summons right in his hand. Problem solved.

Keith knew he had to be on his best behavior if he wanted to see his daughter. He somehow managed to pull himself together one day each week to do that. I had never intended to deprive him of a relationship with Cammy. I only asked for a reasonable amount of normalcy from him.

Keith's father sent him money each week to cover his child-support payments, and then Keith would bring the money to me each time he visited. He also brought Cammy a present each week.

With little else to do, he would videotape hours and hours of cartoons for Cammy to watch. When he came over to visit, he would give the tape to me as a gift for her. Then he would go home and make another tape for his next visit. I did not have the heart to tell him that Cammy had no interest in cartoons and would never watch any of them.

Cammy would be celebrating her first birthday on Tuesday, May 6, 1986.

I had her birthday party on the prior weekend at my parents' house. Friends and family came. Keith did not. He could not bear to face all those people.

He did come to see her on the day of her actual birthday looking the best he had looked in a while; well-dressed as usual but very thin.

He walked into the house carrying a huge box. I don't know how he managed to carry it over.

He sat the box down on the floor and then handed me an envelope. He asked me to please save the card and show it to Cammy when she could read and understand it. He wanted her to always know how much he loved her.

Anxious for Cammy to see her gift, Keith wasted no time in opening the box. He reached in and pulled out a molded-plastic fruit-stand, complete with a cash register, assorted plastic fruit, and little price stakes that fit into holes in each bin.

He could not have given her a more perfect gift. I pictured Cammy looking just like her Daddy as she sold her fruit to make-believe customers.

Keith watched my face to see my reaction. I could see how happy it made him to know that I liked the present. On such a joyous day, just the first of so many happy occasions, it made me sad to think of all he would miss out on.

My child custody case went before a Master on May 22, 1986. We had been legally separated since July 26, 1985. My attorney represented me that afternoon. Keith waived his right to counsel.

After hearing both sides, the court awarded full custody of Cammy to me. That lifted a huge weight off my mind.

The Master awarded Keith two supervised visitations per week, one hour each, at my home. The conditions of visitation were, he could not use drugs unless prescribed by a physician, and he had to furnish my attorney with weekly urinalysis. Both of us were court-ordered to undergo psychiatric evaluations.

Keith told the master his tales of woe concerning his financial situation, failing to mention that he had wealthy parents who supported him and could afford to make substantial child support payments. The Master sympathized with him and only ordered that he pay fifty dollars per week for child support.

I thought he had made a grossly unfair decision. How could anyone, let alone a single mother and child, survive on fifty dollars per week? That made me angry, but it did not overshadow the relief of knowing I had been awarded full custody of Cammy. I could finally stop worrying about her safety.

Glorious Freedom

....

Embrace uncertainty. Some of the most beautiful chapters in our lives won't have a title until much later. ~Bob Goff

....

Five days after the child support and custody hearing, I graduated from the community college Summa Cum Laude with a Certificate of Proficiency in Vision Care.

I had started dating again and had an active social life. I discovered that "normal guys" could be lots of fun.

My focus had changed. I'd had my fill of the cool, charismatic, bad boy type. I hoped to find a nice guy who loved me and my daughter to build a new family with. I wanted Cammy to have a stable daddy to love her and be there for her. I knew it would take a phenomenal man to rise to that challenge. I wondered if he even existed.

Though my life had vastly improved, I grew more and more despondent. Things were not changing fast enough and that frustrated me. I wanted my own home, still had no income, and felt profoundly lonely.

My self-esteem had dropped to an all-time low. I had no confidence that decent guys would have any interest in me once they saw what a mess I had made of my life. I could not imagine things ever getting better.

My girlfriend, Darla, the one who had originally given Keith my number, had separated from her husband shortly after I had separated from Keith. But her situation differed greatly from mine. Her soon-to-be ex-husband had purchased a townhouse for her in a very nice community and kept her comfortable with alimony and child support payments. He also stayed close and involved with their one-year-old son.

Darla invited me to join her on a singles cruise that summer. I would have loved to go along with her but I had no money. As luck would have it, she took the cruise alone and met a nice guy from California.

After the cruise ended, he invited her to visit him in California. She planned to spend two weeks with him there. Since her house would be empty for fourteen days, she offered to let me and Cammy stay there.

I jumped at the chance to get away from my parents and have some privacy. I mostly looked forward to relaxing at the community pool directly across the parking lot from her house. In anticipation, I bought Cammy an inflatable safety tube designed for babies so she could float around the pool with me.

Very few people came to the pool on weekdays. On the weekends, all the young singles living in the community gathered there.

The first Saturday, while relaxing on a lounge chair with Cammy playing on a blanket beside me, I watched two guys enter the pool area. One was taller than the other. The shorter guy had dark hair and a very dark tan. I thought he looked Mexican. They hung around for a while but never looked my way and we never spoke.

Later that day, I decided to go out and get a snowball (a popular Baltimore treat similar to shaved ice and snow cones). I put Cammy in her car seat and drove to the closest snowball stand I knew of.

As I got out of my car, I noticed the shorter, dark-skinned guy I had seen earlier at the pool, talking to the two guys working there. Seeing him up close, I realized he wasn't Mexican, just very tan.

I approached him and mentioned that I had seen him earlier that day at the pool. He said he remembered seeing me there too.

"You're the babysitter who was sitting next to the blond-haired baby on the blanket."

Considering I never saw him look my way, he described the scenario with incredible accuracy.

I started laughing and told him I was the mother, not the babysitter. Then I pointed to the car seat in the back of my car. "That's my daughter, Cammy. My name is Randi."

He told me his name was Billy. Then he introduced me to his younger brother and his brother's friend, co-owners of the snowball stand.

Billy seemed like a nice guy. He asked if my daughter and I would be coming to the pool the following day. I told him we planned to. He mentioned that he and his friends would be hanging out there and invited us to join them.

After I got my snowball, I thanked him and reaffirmed that we would see him the next day at the pool.

When Cammy and I arrived at the pool, Billy greeted us warmly and introduced us to his friends. We spent the entire afternoon at the pool with them and then were invited to join them later at one of their houses.

I had more fun that day than I'd had in years.

Billy and I became good friends. He was twenty-three years old, four and a half years younger than me, but he seemed to have his act together. He already owned his own home in The Falls community.

I definitely felt chemistry between us and we went out on dates a few times, but because of his age, I never considered developing a relationship with him. He did adore Cammy and she liked him too.

After meeting Billy, I met and dated a handful of other single guys living at The Falls. They ranged in age from twenty-three to fifty-something. I had the time of my life.

I never wanted to leave, but I had to. After two weeks, Darla came home from her trip and my party ended.

I dreaded the thought of going back to my parents' house. After two weeks of glorious freedom, I felt tremendously letdown.

Billy and I kept up our friendship and I continued to date a few of the guys I had met at The Falls.

The fifty-year-old guy, a successful real estate agent, divorced with grown kids and fairly well-connected, had taken me out a few times. He probably would have liked to have had a romantic relationship with me, but that did not interest me.

After learning about my financial hardships and legal fees piling up, he offered to help me. He asked his attorney friend if he would represent me in my divorce case Pro Bono. His friend kindly agreed to help me.

No greater gift could have been given to me at the time. I humbly accepted his offer.

There are no coincidences and no random occurrences. Things happen when you least expect them to. Those two weeks at The Falls changed the course of my life—forever.

Gaining Traction

....

*Successful mothers are not the ones that have
never struggled. They are the ones that never gave
up despite the struggles. ~Sharon Jaynes*

....

With the legalities of our separation behind us, Keith no longer had reason to drive a wedge between me and his parents. I kept in touch with them regularly

His parents missed Cammy, the only bright spot in their life. No matter what happened in the future, it seemed we would always have her to bond us together.

Cammy and I flew to Boca in July to visit with them.

Every morning, the three of us rode to the beach club in the Rolls Royce convertible with the top down. Grandpa slept during those hours, so he didn't join us.

We would stay on the beach until naptime. Then I would lay Cammy down to sleep on a palm tree-shaded lounge chair by the pool with "Pill Pill", her favorite little pillow that went everywhere with her.

After a nice day at the beach club, the four of us would dress up and go out to eat. Grandma ordered Cammy all her favorite foods at the restaurants, including lobster.

My in-laws wanted me to find a boyfriend in Florida with the hope that we would ultimately move closer to them. My mother-in-law tried her best to nudge things along. I found that quite ironic after the scene she had made in the restaurant when I had even mentioned moving to Florida someday.

When we went out to dinner each evening, she would approach nice looking guys, ask them if they were single, and then introduce me to them. Typically, the guy would ask if I was her daughter. She would tell him no, I was her daughter-in-law. Then she'd quip, "That's okay, she's divorcing my son!" The guys were left speechless.

We had a wonderful time in Boca. Thankfully, our relationship had survived even though my marriage to their son had not. After two relaxing summer vacations, I looked forward to starting my new career.

I happened to run into a high school friend who I had not seen in ten years. As luck would have it, her fiancé, an Optometrist, would soon be running a brand-new Pearle Vision Eye Lab. She thought he might need a manager for his Optometric office and suggested I call him.

I called him. He contacted the owner and recommended me for the position. The owner interviewed and hired me. Everything fell into place.

The store, still under construction, would open in a few months.

Meanwhile, my new attorney filed the Complaint for Absolute Divorce with the court and sent Keith notification of it. Keith had eighteen days to answer the complaint.

Keith never responded, so my attorney filed a request for an Order of Default. The court scheduled a Master's hearing for February 11, 1987. We had been separated since July 1985 and I could not wait to finalize the divorce.

My youthful sixty-three-year-old father had not worked outside the home in over a year. He never complained, but I knew he needed money and more stimulation. Though I did not like the idea of putting Cammy in day-care, I would consider it under the right circumstances.

I saw a listing from a woman offering day-care in her home and called her.

The woman had one child, a daughter the same age as Cammy, and she wanted one other child to care for. Though only a preliminary screening, I liked what I heard. She sounded like a warm, loving person and very safety-conscious. We arranged to meet at her house.

When I met her face to face, I felt even more comfortable. I liked the way she interacted with Cammy, and the two little girls became instant friends. After spending a few hours chatting and observing, I knew Cammy would be happy, safe, and well provided for there.

The new Pearle Vision Eyelab opened in October and I started working there. I took great pride in having taken my first steps towards independence.

KEITH STRIKES AGAIN

....

Life doesn't have any hands, but it can sure give you a slap sometimes. ~Unknown

....

Before long, the winter holidays were upon us. Keith came over to visit Cammy carrying a shopping bag full of Hanukah gifts. His choices were random, nothing of value but nevertheless thoughtful. Some items still had price tags hanging on them. He had not wrapped anything.

Keith continued his visitations, though I only allowed him to see Cammy when he was sober. He had significantly calmed down. Outside of his once-a-week visits, I had very few dealings with him.

I anxiously counted the days until the finalization of my divorce in February. I hoped for a simple hearing before the Master. I did not even expect Keith to appear or give testimony.

On the day of the hearing, Keith surprised me by strolling into the Master's Chambers at the scheduled time. I had already been waiting there with my attorney, my father, and my best friend, Carolyn, as my witness. Keith had come alone.

The Master took my testimony first. I had filed for divorce on the grounds of voluntary separation. Among other things, I stated that Keith had agreed to the separation and that there was no hope of reconciliation. As my witness, Carolyn backed up my testimony with firsthand knowledge.

When Keith testified, he denied ever agreeing to the separation. He claimed he had asked me to remain with him a number of times.

He also explained to the Master that he had no money, no job, and that his father had to pay his fifty-dollar per week child support.

He admitted to giving daily urinalysis at the drug center but complained that I still refused his visitation rights.

Poor, pitiful Keith solicited the Master's sympathy and manipulated him into taking his side.

In his final report, the Master stated, *"There is a serious question in my mind as to whether or not the defendant can make child support payments as previously ordered, in view of the fact that he hasn't been employed."*

He denied my divorce due to *"reasonable doubt that grounds of voluntary separation existed at the time of separation."*

Keith had screwed me again. I was furious at him for sabotaging the finalization of the divorce. I could not reapply for a hearing for another three months.

Just one week after our divorce hearing, Keith got arrested and locked up on theft charges. The judge sentenced him to one and a half months in the county jail.

During Keith's incarceration, his brother, Mike, who may or may not have been residing at Cliffedge Road, set the house on fire. I don't know how it happened. But the insurance company assessed the damage at fifty-thousand dollars. The house was rendered uninhabitable. Thankfully, I had retrieved everything of value from there when I did.

Besides the disappointment of my thwarted divorce, things were moving in the right direction.

I found a nice two-bedroom apartment in a quiet, older neighborhood. Cammy and I would have the entire first floor of the brick duplex as well as the basement and backyard. It was perfect for us and affordable. I signed the lease.

My parents did not know I had started looking for another place to live. They were not happy when I told them we were going to move.

They wanted to see exactly where we would be living, so I asked the landlord for permission to show the apartment to them before my lease began. I thought they would be excited for me when they saw it.

I was wrong. Between their negative comments and the scowls they wore on their faces from the moment they entered the apartment until they left, they made it crystal clear how unimpressed they were.

They went from room to room picking everything apart, hoping to dissuade me from moving there. My father went down to the basement to look around. He "inspected" the electrical system and found several problems with it. He claimed the house was a fire hazard and he did not want his granddaughter living there.

He did have a valid point about the electrical issues. The wires looked as if they had been jerry-rigged; it would definitely not have passed inspection. But he created so much drama around the problem that we ended up having a huge fight.

I knew that nothing would have been good enough for them. They weren't concerned with the condition of the place—they just did not want me taking Cammy away from them.

Their opinion did not matter to me. Anything was better than living with them. I had made up my mind. We were moving there.

Cammy and I settled comfortably into the apartment and developed our own routine. It felt amazing to have the freedom to raise my daughter without the interference of her overzealous grandparents.

After years of living in chaos, I finally had a peaceful, quiet space to call my own. That meant everything to me.

I felt so proud of myself for how far I had come and how much I had accomplished, against the odds.

With the exception of our impending final divorce, I had little dealings with Keith. I could not wait to be legally free of him.

I blissfully relaxed into my new life, unaware that Hurricane Keith had hit land and was barreling towards me.

With a new job and my own residence, all my personal data had gotten updated and began appearing on my credit report. Since I had excellent credit, I had not given it a second thought.

The credit departments of two major department stores, as well as two major credit-card companies, had gotten nowhere mailing past due statements to Keith's house. Now they knew exactly where to find me.

I began receiving past due bills in my name; itemized statements amounting to several thousand dollars for purchases I had not made and for accounts I had never opened. I felt more and more traumatized with each envelope I opened. It was an inconceivable mess.

As a single parent of a toddler working full-time, living paycheck to paycheck, I had more than enough on my plate. I did not know how I would ever sort it all out.

Though I believed my allegations of fraud would eventually absolve me of all responsibility, I still worried myself sick. I had no idea how long and hard I would have to fight to clear my name.

As I retraced Keith's steps, the deception and violation became more and more appalling.

After I moved from Cliffedge Road, one of the credit-card companies had sent an unsolicited application to me at that address. To initiate the account, they only needed a check mark and signature. Keith checked the box, signed my name, and mailed it back to them, verifying Cliffedge Road as the address. All statements were mailed there without my knowledge.

My allegation of fraud prompted an investigation. Once they determined that the signature on the application was fraudulent, the company apologized to me, closed the account, and absolved me of all charges.

The gas card fraud began in a similar way. Keith had picked up a credit card application at a gas station, filled in my personal

Cliffedge Road

information, and submitted it to the company. The company then approved the application and mailed my credit card to the Cliffedge Road address.

After several months, and a slew of phone calls and certified letters, the gas company deemed the account fraudulent. They still insisted I owed a small portion of the balance. When I refused to pay it, they sent my account to collections.

I had opened a credit account at a department store in the mall, solely in my name, before I had even met him. As far as I knew, Keith was unaware it existed.

He went to the store in person and conned the credit department into allowing him to make purchases on the account that day only. He had them change the address to his so I would not find out what he had done. He managed to do a lot of damage in one day.

Several of Cammy's Hanukah gifts, still with hanging price tags, came from that store. I found them listed on the itemized statement and returned whatever I could. They acknowledged their error and absolved me of all responsibility.

I don't know if Keith remembered we had credit at the other store or just got lucky.

I opened the account in my name and listed Keith as an authorized user when we bought a new refrigerator. I had great credit, he had none at all.

I never gave him a card to use or used the account myself after paying off the appliance. Had I remembered about that joint account, I would have closed it.

It did not matter how hard I fought the charges, they found me completely liable for the debt. I could not afford to pay off the bill so the company issued a judgment against me.

That resulted in ten years of irreparable damage to my credit score.

That S.O.B. had left me homeless and penniless. Now, he destroyed the only thing I had left to fall back on—my credit.

It took months of letters and phone calls to straighten the mess out.

I know it sounds horrible to say, but I wished Keith would drop dead already so I could live my life in peace.

I could think of no other solution.

The Tragic Letter

....

I think it's important to realize you can miss something but not want it back. ~Paulo Coelho

....

Cammy turned two years old on May 6, 1987. I had not heard from Keith in weeks and he didn't come to visit her on her birthday. I did not know the reason why, but it was a relief to not have to deal with him.

On May 7th, he wrote and mailed the following letter to me that explained his absence.

> Dear Randi,
>
> I hope this letter is read before it reaches the trashcan. It's the most sincere hurt I've faced (writing this) straight in years.
>
> I can only start with "if only I had done" but that hardly does much after the way I've disrupted your life, past and future. I would never bother with the puny words "I'm sorry" as that would be like putting a Band-Aid on a broken leg.

As I'm sure you know I'm in Sinai (hospital) with pneumonia. Also, I'm aware everyone realizes my circumstances over the last what seems forever. So, I got my pneumonia from the weakness of my body resistance as I was withdrawing from the pills and methadone. I finally decided after three tries (all with seizures) at coming off Valium that I'd try to do it in the hospital. That was two weeks ago with no signs of getting out. I'm definitely paying the price for my sins.

Randi, it took about a week before I could even begin to scratch the surface of what I did to you. Amazingly, the one particular night that most stands out with the most pain is the night in New York City when you couldn't bring yourself to make love with me. I knew you weren't playing or punishing me, as your honesty wouldn't permit such a game to be played. Later we went to Sardi's Restaurant and I talked the truth. I knew when you couldn't do it with me earlier that our life together would be over unless I did the most drastic event. Tell the truth! And I did! It hurt you <u>so</u> bad. If ever I wanted my life to end, it was then. I still was so much in love with you but I <u>could not stop</u> the drugs. I had to sit and watch that pain in your face. For the last week I've seen that beautiful face every time I can't somehow relax for a little time.

There are so many more times I haven't begun to suffer like I know God is going to make me suffer. If only I could have cried all day in the rehab like I do here, I possibly could have stuck it out drug-free. If only.

I never admitted that it was you I love and miss and need as much as Cammy. I only had to admit that of my child. I can't hide from myself anymore as the doctors have told me my body will not withstand *anymore withdrawals. I'll die from taking the drug or I'd die trying to come off. I know they aren't just scaring me because three different sections of doctors, unrelated, told the same story. My body is equal to that of a 65 year-old man (and I feel like it). Even my mind finally went. Remember how I could count? Give me numbers on paper now and my answer will probably be wrong. If you ask me what I did yesterday you'll get a blank stare.*

In closing, I have of course no illusions of you and I. However, I do have illusions of being a father to my child. Only you can decide if my illusions are just that… illusions. Please consider my desire without thought of revenge. I may not have years to watch <u>our</u> child grow up as my health is so wacked. I would not see her if sickness could in any way spread.

I wish you the happiest of Mother's Day and wish you were not another single mother. I'm certain you are the finest mother in the universe! I wish I was able to be out to get you something, but…I'll make it up.

I <u>still</u> love you,
Keith

I knew that the real Keith, the person I could never stop loving, had written that letter. With tears streaming down my face, I read his tragic thoughts again and again.

I felt compelled to see him. I knew it would probably be the last time.

When I entered Keith's hospital room, his face beamed exactly like it did the very first time he saw me. He thanked me over and over for coming.

Sicker than I had ever seen him but more lucid than he had been in years, he spoke honestly.

I looked at him, wondering for the umpteenth time what torment lie buried deep in his soul. How could someone as lovable as him feel so unworthy of being loved? What drove him to self-mutilate and self-destruct?

I could speculate but would never really know. Sometimes there are no answers. For the sake of my sanity, I had been forced to come to terms with that.

When I left the hospital, I did not know if I would ever see Keith again. The visit gave me the closure I needed.

Keith eventually recovered from the pneumonia and went home. But his body could not take much more abuse. He was a ticking time bomb.

Flipping the Switch

....

There are two kinds of sparks. One goes off with a hitch like a match, but it burns quickly. The other is the kind that needs time, but when the flame strikes...it's eternal. ~Timothy Oliveira

....

I had re-entered the dating scene concerned that having a child would scare men off. A few were uncomfortable with it, mainly the egotistical ones. But for the most part, I wondered who the guys liked more, me or Cammy.

I found no shortage of men to date. The Optometrist I worked with wrote a poem that pretty well summed up my situation, and then he read it at a company party. I will never forget the humorous line: *"With dates for lunch and dates for dinner, does anyone wonder how she keeps getting thinner?"*

The guys I dated were all very nice but not exactly what I hoped to find. I would often complain to my best friend, Carolyn, that I thought I would never find "the one". She kept telling me to be patient.

One day, while Carolyn and I were having one of those discussions, she said to me, "You know you ought to take another look at your friend, Billy. He is very handsome, adores Cammy, and has all the qualities you've been looking for."

I had never considered Billy as husband or father material because of his age, but the more I thought about it, the more sense it made to me.

It seemed she flipped a switch in me and the light in my head turned on. Everything she said was true.

Billy had been right under my nose all along. There could not have been a more perfect guy for me or a better male role model for Cammy.

Billy called me on Memorial Day to ask if I wanted to get together. I told him I had a tentative date but the guy had not called yet. He said, "Blow him off and come out with me." And that is exactly what I decided to do. I knew I would have more fun with my good friend anyway.

Billy picked me up at my house late in the afternoon and we headed to a popular Mt. Washington restaurant/bar to meet with his friends.

As we walked from his car to the restaurant, I reached over and touched his hand. When he took my hand in his, an intimacy we had never before shared flowed between us. No words were necessary. We both knew it was right.

Billy, the oldest of three siblings, had a very close-knit family. I looked forward to the day Cammy and I would get to meet them.

I had already met his brother at the snowball stand but had yet to meet his sister or parents.

One afternoon, he brought Cammy and me to the ranch where his sister rode horses to introduce us to her. His parents happened to be there as well that day so we had the opportunity to meet all three of them.

When I saw the expression on his parents' faces, I knew he had not told them about us yet. It must have shocked them to see their twenty-four-year-old son with a young mother and child. His friendly sister greeted us warmly. His parents acted cordially.

Cliffedge Road

Billy worked with his father in their family-owned business. When he came into the office the next morning, his father questioned him about us. He wanted to know what Billy was doing with that *Shiksa* and her child. Billy laughed and said, "She's not a *Shiksa*, she's more Jewish than we are!"

I did not look Jewish at all and neither did Cammy. People had been telling me I looked like a Shiksa my entire life. Why strangers felt entitled to label me that way, I do not know.

I remember a lady once calling me that to my mother and feeling insulted. I could not have been more than three years old.

One day at the Falls, Cammy and I were in the pool when a Russian lady with an accent swam up to us and commented, "Ah—Shiksa mother, Shiksa baby." I have no idea what caused her to say such a thing to a total stranger.

I grew to like being called a Shiksa. I took it as a compliment and, to this day, proudly wear my Shiksa badge.

After Billy's parents and I got that misunderstanding out of the way, Cammy and I became very close with his family.

His parents loved and treated Cammy as if she were their own granddaughter. His sister and brother became instant aunt and uncle to her.

It turned out that our families had very similar backgrounds and traditions. We discovered that his grandmother and uncle had known me as a little girl before Billy had even been born.

Years back, my grandparents lived in the same neighborhood where Billy's grandparents owned a store. I used to spend a lot of time at their house. My uncle who lived with them would often walk me to Billy's grandparents' store.

It amazed me how perfectly our lives fit together.

Billy could not possibly have loved Cammy more if she were his own flesh and blood. In Cammy's adoring eyes, he was her Daddy. She called him Billy but because she could not say her "L's", it sounded more like "Beewee."

He jumped right into the father role. There was nothing he

wouldn't do for her. He changed her diapers, fed her, and bathed her. If she got tired while we were out, he would carry her across his arms and let her sleep. He sat next to her on the floor of the bathroom while she learned to use the potty, reading book after book to her.

With Cammy's best interests in mind, Keith graciously faded into the background. He somehow knew that Billy had stepped up to the plate and did not want to interfere. I never asked him to stay away. He made that decision entirely on his own. I guess he loved Cammy too much to subject her to the insanity of his life.

Keith's parents remained a constant in our lives. We spoke often. Cammy and I went to Florida and had another wonderful visit with them. I encouraged their involvement in Cammy's life. They were the link to the father she would probably never know.

If it hadn't been for Keith's father, I would have never received any child support. He also paid the tuition for three years of pre-school. I could not have afforded to send her to such a highly accredited private school without his help.

I knew I could always count on his help if I ever needed it. He would have done anything for his granddaughter.

Cammy started pre-school at two and a half years old. Though still very young, she thrived on intellectual stimulation.

She could never soak up enough knowledge. She even spent her playtime in an intellectual way. She learned new things by teaching them to an invisible class.

Cammy met her imaginary playmates, Winnie and Bobbitz, that year. She interacted with them as if they were real. I believe they were guardian angels or spirit guides.

She would carry on long conversations with them while they played together. I had even watched her push them on the swings. They stayed with her until she started elementary school.

Between ages two and three, Cammy developed her signature look, golden-blonde curly hair. She attracted an annoying amount of attention from strangers who thought nothing of touching her head.

Billy had dark curly hair. People often told him how much his "daughter" looked like him. He loved hearing that.

Cammy had found her forever Daddy.

Getting the Get

....

Every great love starts with a great story.
~Nicholas Sparks, The Notebook

....

I received notice in August, after two years and one month of sheer lunacy, that my second divorce hearing had been scheduled.

Keith's whereabouts were unknown. He had not resided on Cliffedge Road since the fire in March and had arranged for the forwarding of his mail to a location undisclosed to me.

The court mailed him notification of the hearing but he never responded.

I appeared before a different Master of the Court on September 10, 1987. Keith, still missing in action, did not show up to the hearing. My revised allegation, two-year separation, could not be disputed.

After the longest twenty-six months of my life, the court finally granted my divorce. Free at last!

Four blissful, Keith-free months passed before I received the following correspondence from his attorney:

Dear Randi,

I received a letter from Keith who is in the Baltimore County Detention Center and he expects to be out around the first of February. He would like to see Cammy upon his release and I would appreciate it if you would give me some dates and times around the first of February for his visitation.

Keith had been sentenced to eighteen months in the county jail again for theft. That explained his absence from the divorce hearing.

Legally, I had to honor his visitation request; fortunately, he never followed through with it.

Cammy and I made plans to go on a one-week vacation to visit her grandparents in Florida that April. Billy arranged to fly down for the weekend and stay at his parents' condo, also in Boca Raton.

Before we went away, he asked me to make reservations at a nice restaurant for our first evening together.

Cammy's grandparents suggested the perfect, quaint Italian restaurant. We had a romantic candlelit dinner.

After dinner, Billy drove me to Deerfield Beach to take an evening stroll along the shore. Above us, the first sliver of the new moon barely lit the night sky. Hand-in-hand in the darkness, barefooted on the cool sand, we paused to share a kiss.

Billy seized the moment. As I watched with astonishment, he slid his hand into his pocket and produced a ring. In concert with the tranquil sound of the rolling surf, he proposed marriage to me. I felt like the luckiest girl in the world.

He handed the engagement ring to me and I placed it on my finger. It fit perfectly. In the darkness, I could not see the brilliance of the diamond, so I pulled him by the hand toward the nearest streetlight. Stupefied by its magnificence, I asked him if it was real. He assured me it was.

The next day, Billy proposed to Cammy. He told her how much

he loved her and wanted to be her Daddy. Then he gave her a tiny diamond "engagement ring" too. He sealed the deal and captured our hearts forever.

Billy hoped to adopt Cammy and become her legal father. I wanted nothing more for both of them but I knew Keith would never consent to forfeiting his parental rights. Though he had no interaction with her, Cammy was the only lifeline he had. If he thought he lost his daughter, he would surely die from a broken heart.

Billy's parents wanted us to have an Orthodox Jewish wedding officiated by the rabbi at their synagogue. I really liked their rabbi and knew he would conduct a beautiful ceremony. But before that could happen, he required me to get a Jewish divorce. Since I had been married before, Jewish law required that I obtain a "Get".

The Get is a religious divorce document presented by the impending ex-husband to his wife. If the man does not initiate the divorce, it is not recognized.

That presented a problem for me. I had no idea where to find Keith. If I found him, he would probably be incoherent. If he was not incoherent, he would just be stubborn. This could not possibly happen.

I explained my situation to the Rabbi. He recommended me to another rabbi who, in complicated situations such as mine, would conduct the Get ceremony without the husband being present. The second Rabbi evaluated my situation and agreed to do it.

When I arrived at the house for the Get ceremony, a man with a long beard, black suit, and black hat answered the door. He invited me into the house where six other men, looking exactly like him, were waiting.

He had me stand and face him and then he started reading something in Hebrew. Suddenly, he scolded me and threw a rolled-up document at me.

I did not understand anything he said, but I figured the harsh tone represented the husband telling the wife he wanted a divorce.

Orthodox men cannot touch any women except for their wife and certain close relatives, which is probably why he threw the document at me instead of handing it to me.

I could not understand or relate to the archaic rituals the rabbi performed and the chauvinistic treatment felt humiliating, but no matter. I left the house with Get in hand.

With that absurd detail out of the way, Billy and I could start planning our wedding. Neither of us liked a lot of fanfare. We wanted an intimate ceremony and celebration.

Anxious to tie the knot, we chose Thursday, July 28, 1988 as our wedding date. We decided to limit our guest list to fifty people; only family and close friends.

I bought a cameo-colored satin and lace dress to wear and had a short veil, per the rabbi's request, made to match it.

I chose a princess style, pastel floral dress for Cammy. It had a white eyelet neckline and a pink satin ribbon around the waist. I bought her silver-colored Maryjane shoes. And I had a small wreath of pink sweetheart roses and baby's breath made for her hair with a matching nosegay to carry.

After having maintained separate residences, I broke my lease and Cammy and I moved in with Billy. We did not plan on staying in that house for very long; we were looking to buy a new one.

Cammy did not feel well on our wedding day, though she did not let on. As we posed for our formal photos before the ceremony, I heard her little voice getting raspy. She was such a good little girl, trying her best to force a smile for the photographer. She never once complained the entire day.

As our guests arrived, Billy, Cammy, and I sat down in the rabbi's study to sign our *Ketubah*. The *Ketubah* is an integral part of a traditional Jewish marriage. The signing of the document by the intended bride and groom always precedes the nuptials.

With the *Ketubah* signed and our guests seated, Billy, Cammy, and I listened outside the sanctuary for our musical cue. Cammy, excited with anticipation, peered through the long glass windows of the chapel's double doors.

When we heard our song playing, the three of us entered the chapel and proceeded down the aisle together. Angelic with the floral wreath nestled in the halo of her golden curls, Cammy stole the spotlight. She self-assuredly sauntered ahead of us, flashing smiles from side to side to all our guests. Only three years old, she really knew how to work a room.

When we reached the end of the aisle, my father lifted her up so she could see everybody, and then sat her down on his lap. Billy and I continued, ascending the steps to the *chuppah* for our wedding ceremony.

The rabbi spoke touchingly about our relationship and our families. He explained the extraordinary significance of our Hebrew wedding date, the fifteenth day in the month of *Av*. According to the Talmud, on that particular date in history, boys and girls of Jerusalem would go out to find a mate. He explained that beautiful marriages were traditionally made on that day.

Standing under the *chuppah*, ready to be joined in holy matrimony, we were given confirmation of what we already knew. Destiny brought us together and 'til death would we part.

A Soft Place to Land

....

It's so easy to fall in love but hard to find someone who will catch you. ~Author Unknown

....

New housing developments were springing up everywhere in Owings Mills, the town just north of Pikesville where we had lived all our lives.

We really liked the model homes in the community Velvet Hills South and ended up buying there. We chose the style we liked and then picked out the lot we wanted to build on.

Billy visited the house nearly every day, from the first time the lot markers went in the ground to the day we moved in. From November 6, 1988 to April 20, 1989, he kept a detailed daily journal and took photographs of each stage of the building process.

I had to pinch myself. Was this "white picket fence" life really mine? It astonished me that I had changed the entire trajectory of my life by changing myself. I had everything I could possibly want.

In Billy, I had found stability, among many other amazing qualities. Drama did not prevail in his world. Before meeting him, I did not know people like that even existed.

He definitely had his quirks just as we all do, but he was a smart guy with his head on straight and his feet planted firmly in the ground. And he had a heart of gold.

I left twenty-nine years of pandemonium behind me. Since childhood, it had been my responsibility to stay strong and hold the people in my life up. I never had the luxury of falling apart. That all changed when I married Billy.

I knew Billy would always be there for me, no matter the circumstance. I had never trusted someone as unequivocally as I trusted my husband.

Finally safe, the emotions I had stockpiled and internalized for my entire life began surfacing as physical symptoms.

It started with my digestive system. Trying to avoid the discomfort I felt after eating, I drastically reduced my food intake. That resulted in substantial weight loss, then overwhelming fatigue.

I consulted with doctors who ran all sorts of tests, including a colonoscopy and endoscopy, but found nothing medically wrong. They attributed my symptoms to stress. No concrete solutions were ever offered. My condition continued to worsen.

When I lost faith in the medical community, I pursued a holistic approach. Desperation led me to a crackpot "healer" that had his own smorgasbord of problems. In addition to his kooky regimens and the recommendation of questionable herbs, he practiced the laying of hands on me. Unaware that his own disharmony could be passed to me by negative energy flowing through his hands, I allowed him to do it. As a result, I got weaker and weaker.

He suggested I see a colonic practitioner. I went to one but the treatments rapidly depleted my already low electrolyte levels and I got much worse. My muscles became so weak I could not get out of bed.

Billy watched me get progressively sicker. A logical problem-solver, he felt helpless in the face of my elusive disorder. He supported me through all the trials and errors and took over for me when I could not function. His devotion to his new bride never wavered.

I suffered for many months, resolving one issue only to have a new one surface. I began experiencing random panic attacks, causing severe hyperventilation that felt like suffocation. Those episodes were terrifying.

My search for wellness eventually led me to healing through the practice of acupuncture and traditional Chinese medicine. The primary function of the ancient art is regulation of the qi circulation (vital energy) to assist the body in self-healing. When a qi meridian is blocked, the body becomes unbalanced. Acupuncture opens the blockages, stimulates the immune system, and balances the emotions.

I had never found a gentler, more comprehensive approach to healing. Acupuncture and Chinese medicine have remained an integral part of my wellbeing ever since.

Though terribly difficult at times, that first challenge so early in our marriage only served to make us stronger as a couple.

Fourth of July

....

The soul leaves its body in search of heaven, leaving behind the pain it faced and entrusting you with their memories. ~Upendra Yadav

....

Keith had only one living grandparent; his maternal grandmother. She thought the sun rose and set with her only two grandsons.

Keith had a close relationship with his grandmother. He genuinely loved her. He could not see her very often because she lived in Florida, but he called her every Sunday.

Mike could have cared less about her. He only buttered her up because he wanted the inheritance.

Keith's grandfather had passed away many years before leaving her very well off. She lived frugally off of her social security income, never enjoying her wealth. Keith's mother, her only child, watched over her.

She and Keith's father managed her money and supervised the planning of her will. They neither wanted nor needed the inheritance. They did not want their addict sons getting their hands on the money and blowing it on drugs.

For years, Keith and Mike's grandmother had been telling them that they would split her money when she died. They did not know that the terms of the original will did not provide for that.

When his grandmother died, Keith's mother learned that her mother had gone behind her back and had a will drawn up to supersede the one they had planned for her. In the new will, she left all her money to her grandsons. Keith's mother disputed the legitimacy of the will and it went into probate for two years.

Keith had told me many times through the years that he thought Mike wanted him dead so he could inherit their grandmother's entire estate. Shortly before he died, Keith told a friend that he knew his brother had tried more than once to kill him with drugs.

As the only heir to Keith's estate, I feared for Cammy's safety. Billy and I kept an unlisted telephone number to make it harder for Mike to find her.

Through my marriage to Billy, Cammy and I gained a wonderful new family. Billy had a wholesome and remarkably close family. His parents were warm, generous, loving people who had raised three outstanding children.

Billy, his sister, and his brother were each other's best friends. And that family bond extended to all their relatives as well. I had never seen anything like it before. His family and extended family loved Cammy as deeply as if she were their own flesh and blood.

Even though we never heard from or saw Keith, my relationship with his parents remained close. I found it challenging to divide my loyalties between my new in-laws and ex-in-laws. The families had nothing in common except their love for Cammy.

My daughter, the only grandchild of three sets of doting grandparents, received a plethora of love and attention. The abundance of love Cammy had in her life far surpassed anything I could have dreamed possible for her.

I only prayed that Keith would not return someday, try to re-enter her life, and turn her world upside down. She had no conscious memory of him, therefore, felt no emotional attachment or loss.

Billy, the only daddy Cammy ever knew and loved, had been there for her since the age of two.

From a very early age, I kept an open dialogue with Cammy about Keith; sharing stories and showing her pictures. I explained that her first Daddy loved her very much but had been too sick to be a part of her life. The older she got, the more detailed my explanations became.

Although I saw no indication of an addictive personality, I wanted her to have a clear understanding of the nature of addiction in case she had a genetic predisposition.

Billy and I discussed having a second child. He said he would be perfectly content with Cammy as his only child. I had always pictured myself with two children.

With Cammy out of diapers and fairly self-sufficient at four years old, I finally had achieved some independence. I did not want to wait too long or become too complacent.

We decided to start trying, knowing with my history that it could take several months for me to conceive.

Cammy had just completed the four-year-old private pre-school program. We looked forward to her starting Kindergarten at our districted elementary school in the fall.

Another summer had arrived. That meant a trip or two to Bethany Beach, Delaware, to stay at the Fine family's condo.

We sometimes planned our trip around the July fourth weekend. Bethany Beach always had a parade during the day and fireworks on the beach at night. That year, we decided to celebrate the holiday at home.

Our friends had an afternoon party at their house. We planned to take Cammy to the park to watch the fireworks later in the evening.

Independence Day fell on a Wednesday that year. July had been an unusually rainy month. Luckily, the weather held out for the holiday festivities and fireworks.

Billy and I gathered up a comforter, some snacks and drinks, and a few card games, and then left home after six p.m. The fireworks usually began around nine, just after dark.

As darkness gradually blanketed the summer sky, the three of us eagerly waited for the fireworks to begin. Suddenly, we heard the familiar-sounding resonant boom, followed by a magnificent burst of shimmering colors that lit up the sky. Thousands of patriotic spectators applauded enthusiastically.

We did not have a care in the world; the three of us snuggled together under the stars on that warm summer night. The future looked bright for our family of three, maybe four someday.

But all wasn't right with the world that night. I had no idea what news awaited me at home.

On July 4, 1990, at thirty-four years old, Keith's tortured soul was called home to rest. He had reached his journey's end.

His brother, Mike, claimed to have found him unresponsive that morning in his bed. No one will ever know what really happened.

According to the autopsy report, he had suffered a fatal overdose due to an acute combination of Methadone, Cyclobenzaprine (Flexeril), and Promethazine (Phenergan).

The imminence of Keith's death did not prepare me for its impact. I took it hard.

Meant to Be

....

It was karma. It was kismet. It was magic. It doesn't matter how it happened, just that it did. ~Shannon Hale

....

Billy waited a respectable six months after Keith's passing to begin adoption proceedings. On April 26, 1991, Cammy, five years old, became Billy's daughter in the eyes of the law. Of course, they did not need that document to prove the depth of their love for each other. He had always been her beloved Daddy and she his precious daughter.

Somewhere in time, we had all made a pact. It was meant to be.

On September 17, 1991, I gave birth to our second child, a son we named Kerry.

The years have flown by. Kerry is now twenty-eight years old and a second-year surgical resident doctor in California.

Billy and I could not be more proud of the intelligent, personable, talented, and level-headed young man he has grown up to be. His future looks extremely bright.

Cammy is now thirty-four years old. There are not enough words of praise to describe the remarkable woman she has become. She has given her family constant joy and pride since the day she was born. Her inner beauty radiates like a golden aura around her as do her tresses of blonde, curly hair.

After eight consecutive semesters on the University's Dean's list, Cammy graduated in 2007, Magna Cum Laude. She is gifted in mathematics and has worked as a data scientist for some of the top corporations in Washington D.C. and New York City.

Cammy's intelligence, maturity, and forthright character have rapidly advanced her as a professional in her career.

Cammy married her wonderful husband, Josh, on September 26, 2016. They both have their master's degrees in data science and are very successful in their careers.

Although Keith never finished high school, he had an extraordinary gift in math and statistics. Astoundingly, he passed all of his positive traits on to Cammy and none of his negative ones.

Cammy has no recollection of ever having known her biological father, though she knows everything about him. She has never felt a loss. Billy was, is, and will forever be her wonderful dad. The two of them are extraordinarily close.

Keith's brother died in 2009 at fifty-nine years old of unknown, drug-related causes. Except for limited and occasional contact with his father, he had been mostly estranged from his parents for many years. For the reasons mentioned in my book, Cammy never knew him.

Cammy, the only grandchild Keith's parents ever had, maintained a close relationship with them until they passed; her grandfather died in 2016 and her grandmother in 2017.

Billy and I have been happily married for thirty-one years. He is an extraordinary husband and father. I could not have dreamed a more perfect man into my life. I am truly blessed.

Postface
Miracles Happen

....

The concept of the marvelous begins to take form when it arises from an unexpected alteration of reality, the miracle. ~Alejo Carpentier

....

One evening in 2008 while watching a news story about the advancements in DNA science, a light went off in my head.

Since DNA profiling did not exist in 1980, the year of my sexual assault, I wondered if my cold case could possibly be reopened and investigated.

I called the Baltimore County Police Department to inquire if they still had the evidence from my rape case. The detective I spoke with looked into it and found out that, unfortunately, the evidence had been discarded.

Having made the call without any expectations, the news did not disappoint me. I never expected them to find the rapist and had been completely resolved about that for thirty years.

In the spring of 2009 while writing the first draft of the original version of this book, I received a telephone call from a Baltimore

County cold-case detective, unprompted and unrelated to my call the year before. I had moved from Maryland to Florida four years prior and he had tracked me down.

Due to the sensitive nature of the situation, the detective respectfully eased into his reason for calling.

He explained that the cold-case department had stumbled upon a miraculous discovery. Someone had found a box containing every pathology slide the forensic doctor who had examined me at the Rape Crisis Center had ever collected. The doctor had died, but he had saved slides from as far back as the 1970s.

The slides were about to be discarded when the cold-case department got wind of them. They applied for and received a million-dollar grant to re-open and investigate the rape cases.

Before reopening a case, they reviewed all the records to determine the legitimacy of them. They had already confirmed the presence of two sets of DNA on my slide and wanted to move forward with the investigation.

The detective told me that most women he had contacted had no interest in revisiting their rape. I could not have been more excited about it. I enthusiastically gave him permission to move forward with the investigation.

In order to determine the perpetrator's DNA code, they had to identify and subtract my DNA code from the mix. But that information would only be beneficial if the rapist had reoffended after 1994, the year the Maryland DNA Database began and fourteen years after my assault.

The detective networked with the police department in Broward County where I currently reside to collect a DNA sample from me.

It should have taken six weeks to get the results but it ended up taking more than five months. In the interim, a female detective took over my case. She stayed in contact with me while we both waited for word from the lab.

In November of 2009, after waiting six months for results, I received a call from the detective. The DNA results had finally come back from the lab.

They had a match.

In most cases, they had to locate the criminal in order to arrest him. Not so in my case. After recently being implicated in another rape case through the same process, he had already been detained in the county jail.

When I learned how brutally the other victim had been treated, I realized just how fortunate I had been.

The fifty-eight-year-old victim had fought for her life. The rapist had severely beaten her and broken her ribs. He tied her hands together, tied a rope around her neck, and hung her upside down in a closet.

The rope around her neck had cut so deeply into her throat, her muscles and larynx were exposed. The man robbed her house and left her for dead.

The victim managed to untie her hands, break loose, and crawl out of the closet. When her thirty-two-year-old son came home, he found her bleeding profusely. The crime-scene photos showed a blood-bath.

Though she survived the attack and lived well into her eighties, she never emotionally recovered from the trauma. She unfortunately never lived to see her attacker identified and arrested. Her son, the only witness to her attack, could only testify to what he saw after the fact.

As the only surviving witness, I had the stronger case to try him on. The Assistant State's Attorney had already charged the man with twelve counts in the other woman's case. Within days of linking him to my crime, she officially charged him with four more counts for my assault. She asked for my approval to prosecute him to the fullest extent of the law.

I learned that the man had been a serial rapist. He had raped three women in the span of fourteen months. I was the first, the woman he had left for dead was the second, and a woman who was later able to identify and prosecute him was the third. With the exception of the rapist who did the crimes, the three cases had no similarities. No behavior pattern could be determined.

In the early 1980s, he had received a thirty-year sentence for the third woman's crime but only served ten. At the time, no one knew of his other two victims.

On February 24, 2010, under the advisement of his court-appointed attorney, the man entered a guilty plea to one count of first-degree rape in relation to my case. DNA evidence is considered indisputable proof. By pleading guilty, he no longer had to face a jury and be tried on all four counts.

On May 20, 2010, the day of his sentencing, I finally got to face the man who had raped and traumatized me thirty years before.

He did not look as menacing as I envisioned he would. I had seen a picture of him in the newspaper prior to the sentencing that looked pretty scary. He had cleaned himself up for court.

He only had his court-appointed attorney with him. No family members or friends showed up to support him.

He looked right at me and listened intently as I read my victim's impact statement, totally engrossed in my words. I wondered if he remembered my voice from thirty years ago.

This is what I said:

> *I want you to know about the girl you violated thirty years ago and the impact your heinous actions had on my life.*
>
> *I was twenty-one years old at the time and looking forward to celebrating my twenty-second birthday in a few weeks. I'd been living on my own for two years. I was young, carefree, and enjoying my newly achieved independence. Life was fun and exciting; I had everything to look forward to. Although my roommate and I hadn't known each other when I'd first moved into her apartment, we had become very close friends*

and were happy living together. Everything changed the night you broke into my home while I soundly slept, terrorized me in my bedroom, threatened my life and raped me.

You were nothing but a coward that night. You deliberately isolated me, leaving me defenseless without any possible way to escape. I couldn't even scream; you held a knife against my throat and I intensely feared for my life. No one was around, and no one would have heard me or could have come to my rescue in time to save me. I didn't know who you were or the degree of your perversion. I didn't know if you possessed even a shred or moral fiber or were psychopathic. And I didn't know if I would live through the night or if you planned to kill me after you'd had your way with me.

You confessed your diabolical plan to me; you told me how you had stalked me and premeditated the attack. How you had been watching me while I unknowingly relaxed outside of my apartment building and talked to my neighbors, naively enjoying my young life. It was a terrifying nightmare that I prayed I'd wake up from…only it *was* real, I *was* awake.

You callously took what you wanted from me without the slightest concern of the way in which your evil-minded actions would impact the rest of my life.

I suspect that you've gone on with your life and never looked back. Thank God I kept a pillow over my head and never saw your face that night. At least I didn't have the horrifying vision of your evil face haunting me for the last thirty years. But my other senses had become heightened, and to this day I remember every detail as if it had happened yesterday.

My whole life fell apart after that night. Besides the residual terror I felt, I was an emotional wreck.

I lashed out at my roommate and moved out shortly after. We've never spoken again. I went into a deep depression and fell on hard times. I isolated myself from friends. Out of despair and confusion, I made some very bad choices in my life.

Not a night has passed in the last thirty years that I haven't woken up between 2 a.m. and 4 a.m., looked at my alarm clock, and remembered what you did to me. That memory will never be erased; it is deeply imbedded in my mind. You stole my right and my ability to feel comfortable alone. Your selfish invasion of my private space thirty years ago has left me feeling forever vulnerable to another attack. I refuse to sleep without the protection of a house alarm, worried that I will once again awake from a sound sleep to an unwelcome and menacing intruder in my bedroom. I'll never again enjoy the cool breeze of the night air through my open bedroom window while I sleep, and have never allowed my children to sleep with their windows open either for fear that someone like you will harm us. That fear will remain with me until the day I die. I will not walk into a home or a building alone unless an alarm system proves to me that no one has entered before me and could be lying in wait. These are the things you forever stole from me that night. I feel vindicated that you've been caught and pray that you will never again have the opportunity to ruin another life.

When I finished reading my victim's impact statement, the judge gave him an opportunity to speak. He continually sobbed as he admitted his crime. He faced me and my family, apologized for the pain he had caused us, and asked for forgiveness. The Assistant State's Attorney told me he probably did not mean a word of it. All criminals say that at their sentencing hearings hoping the judge will go easier on them.

His remorse and apology did not help him at all. The judge sentenced him to life in prison for his crime against me. Already sixty years old, he would die in prison.

To this day, I will not go to bed without first putting the house alarm on and will never leave any windows open. But I am no longer triggered by the memory of the time it happened. That stopped the day of the sentencing.

The solving of my case was nothing short of a miracle. We all experience miracles; some are just more obvious than others.

I now live a peaceful, drama-free life and cherish every minute of it. I gratefully awake each morning with an open mind and an open heart, ready to experience all that life has to offer. And I cannot wait to see what is around the next corner—whatever that may be.

baltimoresun.com

Man awaiting trial for 1981 rape accused in second attack

Baltimore Co. police link suspect to 1980 incident using DNA evidence

By Liz F. Kay | liz.kay@baltsun.com

3:01 PM EDT, October 20, 2009

A Fells Point man awaiting trial for a 1981 rape has been charged with raping a second woman a year earlier, according to Baltimore County police.

In January, Herman Bolling, 58, of the 100 block of S. Broadway was charged in the June 1981 rape and armed robbery of a 58-year-old woman in Reisterstown, said Cpl. Mike Hill, a county police spokesman. Bolling is accused of trying to strangle the woman during an attack that left the victim suffering from broken ribs and a deep cut to her neck, according to police. Armed with a handgun, he also stole about $5,000 worth of property from the woman's home in the 4100 block of Butler Road, police said.

Bolling, who was being held without bail at the Baltimore County Detention Center, is also suspected of raping a 21-year-old woman Aug. 26, 1980, in the 100 block of Village of Pine Court in the Milford Mill community, according to police. The woman was asleep in her home when an intruder put a knife to her throat and raped her, police said.

Detectives reviewing the unsolved Milford Mill case resubmitted evidence from that incident after Bolling's arrest, and his DNA matched, according to police. Bolling has been charged with two counts of first-degree rape, attempted first-degree murder and first-degree burglary, police said.

Copyright © 2009, The Baltimore Sun

Newspaper article about rapist awaiting trial (2009)

Man, 60, sentenced to life in 1980 rape

By Nick Madigan
THE BALTIMORE SUN

A 60-year-old serial rapist was sent to prison for life Thursday after pleading guilty to assaulting a woman in her Randallstown home 30 years ago.

The Aug. 26, 1980, crime, when Herman Bolling awoke a 21-year-old woman and raped her at knifepoint, was linked to Bolling by recently examined DNA evidence. A sexual assault the following year also was connected to him through DNA but was not prosecuted because the victim has since died.

"I owe society for my ill behavior," Bolling told Baltimore County Circuit Judge John G. Turnbull II. But he added, "I am no longer a problem to you or society," and asked for compassion.

Then, turning to the woman he had raped in 1980 and to the son of the woman whom he raped in Reisterstown on June 3, 1981, he said, "I ask that the victims forgive me for my actions."

The 1980 victim said there is "not a night that goes by" when she does not wake up between 2 a.m. and 4 a.m. — about the time the rape occurred — and recall what happened.

Bolling was initially convicted of an Oct. 17, 1981 rape shortly after it occurred. He was sentenced to 30 years in prison and released on July 7, 2005, after serving about 25 years.

Bolling was living in Baltimore when rearrested in January 2009, after DNA evidence linked him to the other two rapes — first the 1980 rape, then the June 1981 crime — said prosecutors Stephanie Porter and Keith Pion.

Before returning Bolling to prison for "the rest of your natural life," the judge described him as "a predator and a danger to society" in the early 1980s. Whether he is "a better person" now will be for a parole board to decide, Turnbull said.

In the June 1981 sexual assault in Reisterstown, police said, Bolling tried to strangle his victim and left her with broken ribs and a deep cut to her neck. She died of unrelated causes in 2006.

nick.madigan@baltsun.com

Newspaper article about rapist life sentence conviction (2010)

Manufactured by Amazon.ca
Acheson, AB